JOHN KNOX
and the Reformation

JOHN KNOX
and the Reformation

D. M. LLOYD-JONES
&
IAIN H. MURRAY

THE BANNER OF TRUTH TRUST

THE BANNER OF TRUTH TRUST
3 Murrayfield Road, Edinburgh EH12 6EL, UK
P.O. Box 621, Carlisle, PA 17013, USA

*

ISBN: 978 1 84871 114 3

*

Typeset in 11.5/16 pt Sabon at the
Banner of Truth Trust, Edinburgh
Printed in the USA by
Versa Press, Inc.,
East Peoria, IL

Remember your leaders,
those who spoke to you the word of God.
Consider the outcome of their way of life,
and imitate their faith.

HEBREWS 13:7

CONTENTS

PUBLISHER'S PREFACE

It is the duty of all Christians to call to remembrance the faithful ministers of God by whom they received the good news about Jesus Christ, the Saviour of the world. For those of Scottish descent no Christian leader deserves more to be remembered than John Knox. Born around 1514, he learned the gospel from the lips of the martyred preacher George Wishart. A reluctant preacher at first, he endured many hardships in order to bring the pure gospel message to a nation in such desperate need of it. Under God's blessing Knox was instrumental in transforming that nation. His stamp, though somewhat faded, still bears its impress upon the Scottish people, both at home and abroad.

This little book is a collection of three addresses. In the first, by the late Dr Martyn Lloyd-Jones, we are shown the reasons why it is so important for the Christian church to remember such historical events as the Reformation in Scotland, in which, of course, John Knox played so significant a role. In the second address (also by Dr Lloyd-Jones), we learn that John Knox was more than a leading figure in the religious history of sixteenth-century Scotland. His influence stretched south of the border too and had a major impact on the Church of England and also on what became known as Puritanism. The last address, a biographical sketch of Knox by Iain H. Murray, takes up what is perhaps the single most dominant theme of Knox's life. It illustrates from the reformer's personal history several important lessons and applies them in a helpful way to the life of Christians today.

As we approach the five hundredth anniversary of the birth of John Knox, may this book encourage readers not only to remember him but also to consider the outcome of his life and to imitate his faith (*Heb.* 13:7).

JOHN KNOX
Timeline

Knox Flees Persecution — Ministers in Europe

Knox's Last Years in Scotland

REMEMBERING
THE REFORMATION

D. M. LLOYD-JONES

Mr Chairman and Christian friends, I would like to say immediately that I regard this occasion as one of the greatest privileges that has ever fallen to my lot.[1] I prize the invitation that I received from the friends of the Free Church of Scotland very highly indeed. This is an historic occasion. We are doing something that I am certain is well pleasing in the sight of God and which I trust, under God's benediction and blessing, will prove to be of value and of benefit to our souls and, let us hope, to the whole cause of God in this nation and in all nations at this present time. I always say, when I have the pleasure of coming to Scotland, that I am interested to come, not only because of my concern about the gospel, but because of the deep feeling of admiration which I have always had within me for you as a nation and as a people. And there is certainly nothing in your long history which is more glorious and

[1] The report of an address given in the Usher Hall, Edinburgh on 5 April, 1960, in commemoration of the 400th Anniversary of the Reformation in Scotland.

more remarkable than that great movement of God which took place four hundred years ago, and which we are met tonight to commemorate. Therefore, for every reason I was very ready to come here to Edinburgh once more.

Now our Chairman has very rightly put to you one of the questions that I also felt should be put, because it is a question which does arise, apparently, in the minds of some people. Why, they wonder, should we consider the Reformation in Scotland at all at a time like this, with the world as it is and with the multiplicity of problems that are pressing in upon us on all sides? Why turn back and consider what happened four hundred years ago?

As I understand it there are two main objections to doing this. The first is a *general objection to looking back*, a feeling that the past has nothing to teach us. For, after all, we are the people of the twentieth century, the people who have split the atom, who are encompassing all knowledge and have advanced to such giddy heights as our forefathers could not even have imagined. Why then should we, of all people, look back, and especially look back four hundred years? The whole climate of opinion today, and indeed during the last hundred years, has been governed by the evolutionary theory and hypothesis, which holds that man advances from age to age and that the present is always better than the past; this whole climate of thought is inimical to the idea of looking back and learning from previous history. That is one objection.

The other objection is that we should not hold a meeting like this because *the Reformation was a tragedy*. Now this is a view which is gaining currency very rapidly at present. We are told that what we should be considering today is unity, and that if we spend our time considering the disruption and division in the church which took place four hundred years ago, we are doing something sinful. There is, alas, an increasing body of opinion in Protestant circles which is saying, openly and unashamedly, that the Protestant Reformation was a tragedy and that it is our business to forget it as soon as we can and to do everything possible to heal the breach, so that we shall be one again with the Church of Rome, and there shall be one great world church.

Those are the two commonest objections, as I see the situation, which are brought against what we are engaged in doing this evening. Why then are we doing it? How do we justify a gathering such as this, and the other gatherings that are to follow?

Well, let me say quite frankly that there are wrong and false ways of doing what we are doing here tonight. There are people who are interested in the past merely in an antiquarian sense; history happens to be their great interest in life. They like delving into the past and reading about the past, not that they are interested in it in any kind of active philosophic or religious sense; they just like burrowing in ancient history. There are people who do this in other realms; some like collecting old furniture, and the glory of anything to them is that it is old. They are not interested in a chair from the standpoint of something to sit upon; what they are interested in is the age of the chair. Now that is antiquarianism, and it is possible for us, of course, to be governed by a purely antiquarian or historical motive. But there is no value in that; the times in which we are living are too urgent and too desperate for us to indulge a mere antiquarian spirit.

Now the last time I stood at this desk, I said that I could not speak without having a text. Well, I am still the same. And it seemed to me that there were two texts which would not be inappropriate for this meeting, and for our consideration this evening. There is a right way and a wrong way of viewing a great event like the Reformation and the great men who took part in it. The first, the right way, we are told of in the Epistle to the Hebrews, chapter 13, verses 7 and 8: 'Remember them which have the rule over you, who have spoken unto you the word of God: whose faith follow, considering the end of [or, the outcome of, their lives and of] their conversation. Jesus Christ the same yesterday, and today, and for ever.' That is the right way to do it; *we look at these men in order that we may learn from them, and imitate and emulate their example.*

But there is a wrong way of doing this, and we find it in Matthew, chapter 23, verses 29-33. These are terrible and terrifying words: 'Woe unto you, scribes and Pharisees, hypocrites! because ye build the tombs of the prophets, and garnish the sepulchres of the righteous, and say, If we had been in the days of our fathers, we would not have been partakers with them in the blood of the prophets. Wherefore ye be witnesses unto yourselves, that ye are the children of them which killed the prophets. Fill ye up then the measure of your fathers. Ye serpents, ye generation of vipers, how can ye escape the damnation of hell?'

Now those are the words of the Lord Jesus Christ and he was addressing his own generation, his own contemporaries. He said, in effect, You are paying great tribute to the memory of the prophets; you are looking after and garnishing their sepulchres and you are saying what great men they were — how noble, how wonderful, we must keep their memory alive — and you say what a terrible thing it was that your forefathers should have put these men to death. If you had been alive then, you maintain, you would not have joined them in those wicked deeds; you would have listened to the prophets, you would have followed them. You hypocrites, says our Lord, you would have done nothing of the sort.

How, then, does he prove it? Well, he does it in this way. He tests their sincerity by discovering what their attitude is at the present to the successors to the prophets. What is their reaction to the people who are still preaching the same message as the prophets? He says, You say that you are admirers of the prophets and yet you are persecuting and trying to compass the death of a man like myself who is the modern representative of the same message, and the same school of prophecy. Ah, says our Lord, it is one thing to look back and to praise famous men, but that can be sheer hypocrisy. The test of our sincerity this evening is this: What do we feel about, and how are we treating, the men who, today, are preaching the same message as was preached by John Knox and his fellow reformers?

So, you see, this meeting is a very important one for us. You cannot do a thing like this without examining yourself, without coming under scrutiny. Our presence indicates that we are admirers of these great prophets of God, but I wonder whether we are in reality? So it is a good thing, it seems to me, that we should come together, if only so that we can examine ourselves in the light of this word of our Lord and Saviour Jesus Christ.

Why then are we doing this? How do we justify our action? Our Chairman has already dealt with one of the answers. The fact is that *you simply cannot understand the history of Scotland unless you know something about the Protestant Reformation.* It is the key to the understanding of the history of your great country in the last four hundred years. What Scotland has been she has been, directly and unmistakably, as a result of the Protestant Reformation. So if we had no other reason, that is enough.

You are a nation of people famous for education, for knowledge, for culture. Everybody knows that. The peasants of Scotland were cultured and able, intelligent and intellectual people. What accounts for that? It is not merely a matter of blood, because before the Protestant Reformation they were woefully ignorant, backward, and illiterate. What is it, then, that has caused your nation to be regarded, perhaps by the whole world, as supreme in her interest in education and the pursuit of knowledge? The answer is, the Protestant Reformation. So, apart from any religious considerations we have this mighty and all-important consideration.

And then I want to add a third reason. Why are we considering the Reformation of four hundred years ago? Well, if I am to be quite honest, I must confess that this is my main reason: *because of the state of affairs today*. I am primarily a preacher, not a lecturer, not an historian, very fond of history, but not an antiquary, as I have said. No, I am interested in this because, as a preacher, I am concerned about the present state of affairs which is increasingly approximating to the state of affairs that obtained before the Protestant Reformation. You are aware of the state of the morals of this country, and of Great Britain in general, before the Reformation: vice, immorality, sin were rampant. My friends, it is rapidly becoming the same again! There is a woeful moral and social declension. We are being surrounded by the very problems that were most obvious before the Reformation took place. The moral state of the country, these urgent social problems, juvenile delinquency, drunkenness, theft and robbery, vice and crime, they are coming back as they were before the Protestant Reformation.

But it is not only a matter of moral and of social problems. What of the state of the church? What of the kirk? What about the numbers who are members of the church? How many even attend? We are going back to the pre-Reformation position. What about the authority of the church? What about the state of doctrine in the church? Before the Reformation there was confusion. Is there anything more characteristic of the church today than doctrinal confusion, doctrinal indifference — a lack of concern and a lack of interest? And then perhaps the most alarming of all, the increase in the power, influence, and numbers of the Church of Rome, and the romanizing tendencies that are coming into and being extolled in the Protestant church! There is no question about this. This is a mere matter of fact and observation. There is an obvious tendency to return to the pre-Reformation position; ceremonies and ritual are increasing and the Word of God is being preached less and less, sermons are becoming shorter and shorter. There is an indifference to true doctrine, a loss of authority, and a consequent declension, even in the matter of numbers. I wonder, Christian people, whether I am exaggerating when I suggest that at the present time we are really engaged in a great struggle for the very life of the Christian church, for the essence of the Christian faith? As I see the situation, it is nothing less alarming than that. We are fighting for an heritage, for the very things that were gained by that tremendous movement of four hundred years ago. That to me is the most urgent reason. We cannot afford the luxury of being merely antiquarian; we should be concerned about this because of the state of affairs in which we find ourselves.

But, somebody might say, why go back for the answer to that? Why don't you do what is being done everywhere else, and in every other realm of life? I read an article in a supposedly evangelical weekly paper not so long ago, which said, 'Why does the Church stand still?' The man went on to say something like this: 'I see in business and everywhere else that people are making experiments, they are employing the backroom boys and the experimenters, and they are trying to discover new methods, new machinery, new everything — Why doesn't the Church do this? The Church always seems to be looking back.' They regard that as something which is wrong. Now the answer to that, as I see it, can be put like this. I am not at all sure but that the greatest of all the lessons which the Protestant Reformation has to teach us is just this, that the secret of success in the realm of the church and of the things of the Spirit, is to go back. What happened in essence four hundred years ago was that these men went back to the first century, they went back to the New Testament, they went back to the Bible. Suddenly they were awakened to this message and they just went back to it. There is nothing more interesting, as one reads the stories of Luther and of Calvin, than to notice the way in which they kept on discovering that they had been rediscovering what Augustine had already discovered, and which had been forgotten. Indeed I suggest that perhaps the greatest of all the lessons of the Protestant Reformation is that the way of recovery is always to go back, back to the primitive pattern, to the origin, to the norm and the standard which are to be found alone in the New Testament. That is exactly what happened four hundred years ago. These men went back to the beginning, and they tried to establish a church conforming to the

New Testament pattern. And so, let us be guided by them, as we look at them this evening and as we try to garner certain lessons from them.

What, then, happened four hundred years ago? Well, whatever your views may be, you will have to admit that it was one of the most remarkable historical phenomena that have ever taken place. It is no exaggeration to say that the Protestant Reformation changed and turned the entire course of history, not only the history of the church but secular history too. There is no question about this, and it is granted by historians, that the Reformation laid the foundation of the whole democratic view of government. That is a fact of history. All the nations of the world at present are looking to the United States of America. How did the United States of America ever come into being? It would never have come into being were it not for the Protestant Reformation. The Puritan fathers who crossed the Atlantic in the Mayflower were men who were products of the Reformation, and it was the desire not only for religious liberty, but also for democratic liberty, that drove them to face the hazards of crossing the Atlantic at that time and to establish a new life, a new state, and a new system of government in the New World. You cannot explain the story of the United States of America except in terms of the Protestant Reformation.

The Reformation gave life-blood to the whole democratic notion in the realm of politics, and the consequences, as judged from a social and from a moral standpoint, simply baffle description. This country of yours, from being a dissolute, drunken, and illiterate country, became famous throughout the world for her sober, righteous, able, intelligent people. And it was the Protestant Reformation that led to it.

My difficulty on this occasion is to know what not to say. The theme as you see, is endless. But let me interject this before I proceed, for it is one of the greatest lessons which need to be learned at the present time. Everybody today is aware of the moral problem, and they are trying to deal with it along various lines: acts of Parliament, prison reform, psychiatric treatment in the prisons, and the various other expedients which are advocated. But they do not seem to be very successful, do they? Why not? For the reason that you cannot have morality without godliness. The tragedy of the last hundred years has been due to the fallacy of imagining that you could shed Christian doctrine but hold on to Christian ethics. That has been the controlling notion. But it cannot be done. There is one verse in Paul's Epistle to the Romans, chapter I, verse 18, which should have put us right on this once and for ever: 'For the wrath of God is revealed from heaven against all ungodliness and unrighteousness of men.' You notice the order - ungodliness first, unrighteousness second. If you do not have a godly people, you will never have a righteous people. You cannot have righteousness without godliness. And the Protestant Reformation is the most striking proof of this that the world has ever known. Once you have godliness, righteousness and morality follow. We are today trying to have morality, righteousness, and a good ethical conception without the godliness, and the facts are proving, before our eyes, that it simply cannot be done. So if you are a sociologist in this meeting, if you are a politician, if you are just interested in the moral problem, then I say to you, go and read the history of the Reformation. There you will see that the only way to exalt your nation is to put godliness first, and righteousness will then follow.

As I have said, the Reformation was not purely a religious movement. It was a general movement and it was witnessed, not only in Scotland, but in England, France, Holland, Switzerland, Germany, and various other countries on the Continent. It was a great movement of the Spirit of God in which your country was given her share and portion.

Well, what do we find as we look at it? I can only give you some headings. If you want the details, I commend to you very warmly and happily the book by our Chairman, which has already been mentioned to you.[2] It gives a clear, succinct account of what actually happened, and it is a thrilling and moving story. Buy it, read it, and digest it. He gives you the general setting and shows you the peculiar features in Scotland. The one excellence, of course, which we who come from south of the border have to grant you is that your reformation was a pure reformation. In Scotland, there was no question of a king trying to get out of his matrimonial difficulties and entanglements. You were free of that. It was a pure reformation and the result was, I believe, that you had a purer church. But, generally speaking, what happened here was the same as what happened in most other countries.

What do we see then? Well, of course the first thing that attracts our attention is the men, the men

[2] A. M. Renwick, *The Story of the Scottish Reformation* (London: IVF, 1960). Currently available from Christian Focus Publications.

that God used. Look at them, Patrick Hamilton, George Wishart, John Knox, Andrew Melville, John Welsh, and many others. Here are men worthy of the name! Heroic, big men, men of granite! Our Chairman need not apologize for being a history worshipper, I am a hero worshipper! Think what you like of me, I like to look at and to read of a big man! In an age of pygmies such as this, it is a good thing to read about great men. We are all so much alike and of the same size, but here were giants in the land, able men, men of gigantic intellect, men on a big scale in the realm of mind and logic and reason. Then look at their zeal, look at their courage! I frankly am an admirer of a man who can make a queen tremble! These are the things that strike us at once about these men. But then I suppose that the most notable thing of all was the fact of the burning conviction that dwelt within them; this is what made them the men they were.

What were these convictions? What did these men believe? What did they teach? What were their characteristics? Here is the first, obviously: their belief in *the authority of this Book*. The pre-Reformation church was moribund and asleep under a scholastic philosophy that displayed great cleverness, with intellectual and critical acumen. But it

was all in the clouds and dealt with vague gener-
alities and concepts, while the people were kept in
utter ignorance. The men who did the teaching and
the lecturing argued about philosophic concepts,
comparing this view with that, and indulging in
refinements and minutiae. But, in contrast, the great
thing that stands out about the reformers was that
they were men who went back to the Bible. They
said, nothing matters but this. This, they said, is
the Word of God in the Old Testament and in the
New Testament, this is not theory, supposition, or
speculation, this is the living God speaking to men:
he gave his Word to the prophets, they wrote it; he
gave it to the apostles, they recorded it; and here
it is for us. Here we have something which is in a
category of its own, the living Word of God speaking to men about himself, about men, about the
only way they can come together and live together.
They stood for the authority of the Bible, not for
scholastic philosophy.

You see, my friends, the importance of looking
back at the Reformation. Is not this the greatest
need at the present time, to come back to this
Word of God? Is this authoritative or is it not?
Am I in any position to stand above this Book, and
look down at it and say, That is not true, this or

that must come out? Is my mind, is my twentieth-century knowledge the ultimate judge and decider as to the veracity of this teaching? It is since the time, a hundred years ago, when that notion began to creep in, that the church has been going down. But the reformers based everything upon this Book as the Word of God to man, which they were not to judge but to preach. And you and I have got to return to this. There can be no health, there can be no authority in the church, until she comes back to this basic authority. It is idle to talk about this as the Word of God in a sense which still allows you and me to decide that certain things in it are not true! The Book hangs together. The Lord Jesus Christ believed the Old Testament. After his resurrection, he took his disciples through the books of Moses and the Psalms and the Prophets. He says, I am there, let me show you myself there. Read them, why have you not understood them? Why have you not believed all that the prophets have written? That was their trouble, it has always been the trouble of the church in periods of declension, and we must come back to the Protestant reformers' position and recognize that we have no authority apart from the authority of this Word of God.

In this Book they found also the mighty doctrine of *the sovereignty of God,* which taught them not to approach their problems in a subjective manner as you and I are prone to do. Their concern was not, how can I get a bit of help, how can I get some physical healing, how can I get guidance, how can I get happiness and peace, how can I get a friend who will help me in my loneliness? No, they saw themselves before this almighty, sovereign God and the one question was, How can a man be just with God? They bowed before him! They were godly men; they were God-fearing men. God was at the centre of their thoughts, the controller of their activities and their lives. The sovereignty of God! They did not talk much about free will, as I read them, but they knew that God was over all, and he was to be worshipped and to be feared.

And then there was *the great central doctrine of the Lord Jesus Christ and his perfect finished work.* They did not feel sorry for him as they looked at him on the cross, they saw him bearing their sins, they saw God laying on him the iniquity of us all, they saw him as a substitute, they saw God putting our guilt upon him and punishing him for our guilt. The substitutionary atonement! They preached it; it was everything to them. The finished, complete, atoning work of Christ. They gloried in it! And that in turn, of course, led to the great pivotal central doctrine of which we were reminded in the reading, *justification by faith only.*

Now, I may be mistaken, but as I see the contemporary situation, the greatest battle of all, perhaps, at the moment is the battle for justification by faith only. 'Works' have come back! I was reading a religious newspaper a fortnight ago which carried the words 'Saint Gilbert' as a heading to a paragraph. The writer of the paragraph was of the opinion that this man whose Christian name was Gilbert was undoubtedly a saint and we must accord him the name and the dignity of a saint. Then he went on to say this: 'Of course I know that in actual practice he called himself a rationalistic agnostic.' Though this man Gilbert called himself a rationalistic agnostic, a so-called Christian paper says that nevertheless he was a saint. And they justified their assertion on the basis of his life: he was a good man, he was a noble man, he had high and exalted ideals, he gave much of his life to the propagation of the League of Nations union, and to uplift the human race, he tried to put an end to war, he made protests against war; therefore, the argument goes, though he denied the being of God, though he did not regard the Bible as the Word of God, though he did not believe in the Lord Jesus Christ, nevertheless, he was a saint. What makes a man a saint? Oh, his works, his life!

We are confronted again by a generation that no longer believes in justification by faith only; we are told that 'the greatest Christian' of this century is a man whose belief in the deity of Christ, to put it at its mildest, was very doubtful, who certainly did not believe in the atonement, whose creed seemed to be what he calls 'reverence for life' — yet we are told that he is the greatest saint and Christian of the twentieth century! Look at his life, they say, look what he has done; he gave up a great profession and he has gone out to Central Africa, look what he has suffered, look what he has given up, he might be wealthy, he might be prosperous, but he is living like Christ, he is imitating Christ, he has done what Christ has done! You see, it does not matter what you believe. According to this teaching, it is the life that makes a man a Christian. If you live a good life, if you live a life of sacrifice, if you try to uplift the race, if you try to imitate Christ, you are a Christian, though you deny the deity of Christ, though you deny his atonement, though you deny the miraculous and the supernatural, the resurrection and many other things, nevertheless you are a great Christian and a great saint!

My friends, John Knox and other men risked their lives, day after day, just to deny such teaching and to assert that a man is justified by faith alone without works, that a man is saved not by what he does but by the grace of God, that God justifies the ungodly, that God reconciles sinners unto himself. It is all of God and none of man, and works must not be allowed to intrude themselves at any point or in any shape or form. The battle for justification by faith only is on again! And if this meeting and these celebrations do nothing else, I trust that they will lead us to a rediscovery of the absolute centrality of the doctrine of justification by faith only.

These reformers were also men who believed in *possessing assurance of salvation*. Now I am somewhat more controversial, am I not? Do you believe in assurance of salvation as the Protestant reformers did? I have known people who have paid great tribute to the memory of John Knox and others, who deny the possibility of assurance and regard it as almost an impertinence. I know that the *Westminster Confession of Faith* is careful to say that a man can be saved without assurance of salvation, that saving faith and assured faith are not the same thing, and I am happy to agree with the *Westminster Confession*. But let me say this: the Protestant reformers were so against the Roman Catholic Church, which teaches that a man can never be certain, that they did not draw that distinction, and they would have been equally against a modern movement, which likes to claim itself as reformed, but which denies the possibility of assurance. These Protestant reformers said that a man was not truly saved unless he had assurance! Without going all the way with them, we must notice this, that whenever the church is powerful and mighty and authoritative, her preachers and ministers have always been men who speak out of the full assurance of faith, and know in whom they have believed. It was for that reason that the martyrs could smile in the face of kings and queens, and regents and local potentates, and go gladly to the stake; they knew that from the stake they would wake in heaven and in glory and see *him* face to face! They rejoiced in the assurance of salvation!

Then, to make my little list complete, I must add a few more of their main convictions. They were men who believed in *the universal priesthood of believers*. They held to *simplicity of worship*. Away with idols, away with vestments, away with forms and ceremonies. A simple service! And not least important, *a pure church*. The three marks of the church that they taught are these: it is a place where the pure gospel is preached, where the sacraments are administered, and where discipline is exercised. A pure church! No room for all and sundry; no room for men who are doubtful, no room for men who show by their lives that they love the world and its ways and its sin. No! A pure church, because the church is the body of Christ! Those were their convictions, those were the doctrines which they held.

The other thing I want to note about them is this: *their power in prayer*. We must not think of these reformers only in terms of doctrine, though we must start with that. This other thing was equally notable and remarkable about them, they were men of prayer. Did not Mary, Queen of Scots fear the prayers of John Knox more than she feared the English soldiers? Of course she did! Why? Because he was a powerful man in prayer. Have you read about the prayer life of John Welsh, the son-in-law of John Knox? There was a man who spent nights in prayer; his wife would wake up at night and find him on his knees almost stone-cold. What was he doing? Praying for the townspeople to whom he was ministering, asking for power, asking for authority. These men, everyone of them, were men of great prayerfulness; they spent hours of their lives in prayer, knowing that in and of themselves, though their doctrines were right and orthodox, they could do nothing. I like to hear that story of another of these men, Robert Bruce. We read that when he was praying with some ministers one day, he felt they were lifeless and dull. He cried to God that the Holy Spirit might come down upon them but nothing seemed to be happening. Then as he began banging on the table they were all conscious of God coming among them and thereafter men spoke of Bruce as one who knocked down the Holy Ghost among them! Is not that the kind of man we need today? Where is the power, where is the influence, where is the authority? These reformers were only men like us but they knew these things. They were men of prayer, who lived in the presence of God and who knew they could do nothing without him.

This brings me to the last point: *their preaching*. We have been reminded that the reformers re-introduced preaching and that they put preaching at the centre instead of ceremonies and sacraments. Yes, but let us remember that there is preaching and preaching. Merely to speak for twenty minutes is not necessarily preaching. Though you may have taken a text and divided it up very cleverly, it is not necessarily preaching. Oh, there is preaching and preaching! What is the test of preaching? I will tell you; it is power! 'Our gospel came unto you', says the apostle to the Thessalonians in the First Epistle, chapter 1, verse 5, 'not in word only, but also in power, and in the Holy Ghost, and in much assurance.' Who had the assurance? The preacher! He knew something was happening, he knew God was using him, he knew that he was the vehicle and channel of divine and eternal grace. 'Much assurance'! And that was the sort of preaching you had from the Protestant reformers. It was prophetic preaching, not priestly preaching. What we have today, is what I would call priestly. Very nice, very quiet, very ornate, sentences turned beautifully, prepared carefully. That is not prophetic preaching! No, what is needed is authority! Do you think that John Knox could make Mary, Queen of Scots tremble with some polished little essay? These men did not write their sermons with an eye to publication in books, they were preaching to the congregation in front of them, anxious and desirous to do something, to effect something, to change people.

It was authoritative. It was proclamation, it was declaration.

Is it surprising that the church is as she is today; we no longer believe in preaching, do we? You used to have long sermons here in Scotland. I am told you do not like them now, and woe unto the preacher who goes on beyond twenty minutes! I was reading in the train yesterday about the first Principal of Emmanuel College in Cambridge—Chadderton—who lived towards the end of the sixteenth century. He was preaching on one occasion, and after he had preached for two hours he stopped and apologized to the people: 'Please forgive me, I have got beyond myself, I must not go on like this.' And the congregation shouted out, 'For God's sake go on!' You know, I am beginning to think that I shall not have preached until something like that happens to me. Prophetic! Authoritative! Proclamation! Declaration! Their view of preaching was certainly not our modern idea of having a friendly discussion. Have you noticed how we have less and less preaching on the wireless [radio] programmes? Instead we have discussion. Let the young people say what they think, let us win them by letting them speak; and we will have a friendly chat and discussion, we will show them that after all we are nice, decent fellows, there is nothing nasty about us; and we will gain their confidence; they must not think that we are unlike them! If you are on the television you start by producing your pipe and lighting it; you show that you are like the people, one of them! Was John Knox like one of the people? Was John Knox a matey, friendly, nice chap with whom you could have a discussion? Thank God he was not! Scotland would not be what she has been for four centuries if John Knox had been that kind of man. Can you imagine John Knox having tips and training as to how he should conduct and comport himself before the television camera, so as to be nice and polite and friendly and gentlemanly? Thank God prophets are made of stronger stuff! An Amos, a Jeremiah, a John the Baptist in the wilderness in his camel-hair shirt—a strange fellow, a lunatic, they said, but they went and listened to him because he was a curiosity, and as they listened they were convicted! Such a man was John Knox, with the fire of God in his bones and in his belly! He preached as they all preached, with fire and power, alarming sermons, convicting sermons, humbling sermons, converting sermons, and the face of Scotland was changed: the greatest epoch in your long history had begun!

There, as I see it, were the great and outstanding characteristics of these men. What was the secret of it all? It was not the men, as I have been trying to show you, great as they were. *It was God!* God in his sovereignty raising up his men. And God knows what he is doing. Look at the gifts he gave John Knox as a natural man; look at the mind he gave to Calvin and the training he gave him as a lawyer to prepare him for his great work; look at Martin Luther, that volcano of a man; God preparing his men in the different nations and countries. Of course, even before he produced them, he had been preparing the way for them. Let us never forget John Wyclif and John Hus; let us never forget the Waldensians and all the martyrs of these terrible Middle Ages! God was preparing the way; he sent his men at the right moment, and the mighty events followed.

Shall I try to draw certain lessons for ourselves? The conclusion of all this is that *righteousness, and righteousness alone, exalts a nation, and there is no righteousness without a preceding godliness.* The times are cruel; the world is in a desperate plight; there is an appalling moral breakdown before our eyes. Marriage is breaking down, home life disappearing, little children not knowing home and loving parents. It is a tragedy! Can nothing be done? Is there no hope? To me the main message of the Protestant Reformation of four hundred years ago is to point us to the one and only hope. Things were bad in Scotland when God called John Knox and sent him out as a burning flame and the others with him. Our position is not hopeless, for God remains, and with God nothing shall be impossible! The conditions could not have been worse than they were immediately before the Reformation; yet in spite of that the change came. Why? Because God was there and God sent it. So the only question we need ask is the old question of Elisha face to face with his problem: 'Where is the Lord God of Elijah?' And I want to ask that question this evening: *Where is the God of John Knox?* Our meeting will have been in vain if we do not ask that question. If we stop with John Knox it is not enough; the question is, Where is the God of John Knox, he who can give us the power, the authority, the might, the courage, and everything we need, where is he? How can we find him? I suggest to you that the answer is to be found again in the Epistle to the Hebrews, in chapter 4 this time, in verses 14 to 16. They seem to me not inappropriate as I end this evening.

How can we find this God? Here is the answer: 'Let us hold fast the confession.' It does not actually mean there, of course, the *Westminster Confession*, though in reality it does! Hold fast the old *Scots Confession*. You will never find the God of John Knox without that. 'Seeing then that we have a great high priest that is passed into the heavens, Jesus the Son of God, let us hold fast the confession . . .' What is the confession? It is the confession about 'Jesus the Son of God', our great high priest; the *Scots Confession*, the *Westminster Confession*, the faith of these Fathers. We must have it because without it, who dares go into the presence of God? As it is put there in Hebrews 4:16: 'Let us therefore come boldly unto the throne of grace . . .' What is the 'therefore'? The knowledge that we possess, that we have got this great high priest that has passed through the heavens, Jesus the Son of God, and that he is 'touched with the feeling of our infirmities, but was in all points tempted like as we are, yet without sin.' Where is the God of Elijah? How can we find him? How can we receive the power that we need? We must go back to the confession, go back to the faith, go back to the Word, believe its truths, and in the light of it go with boldness, confidence, assurance, to the throne of grace; to obtain mercy and find grace to help in time of need. We are living in an appalling time of need, sin and evil rampant;

the whole world is quaking and shaking. Is the end upon us? The times are alarming—'time of need'. The one thing necessary is to find this God, and there seated at his right hand, the One who has been in this world and knows all about it, has seen its shame, its sin, its vileness, its rottenness face to face; friend of publicans and sinners, a man who knew the hatred and the animosity of the Pharisees, scribes and Sadducees, the doctors of the law, and Pontius Pilate. The whole world was against him, and yet he triumphed through it all; he is there, and he is our representative and high priest. Believe in him, hold fast to the confession. Let us go in his name with boldness unto the throne of grace, and as certainly as we do so we shall obtain the mercy that we need for our sinfulness and unfaithfulness, and we shall be given the grace to help us in our time of need, in our day and generation. The God of John Knox is still there, and still the same, and thank God, Jesus Christ is the same yesterday, today, and for ever. Oh, that we might know the God of John Knox!

JOHN KNOX:
THE FOUNDER OF PURITANISM

D. M. LLOYD-JONES

Most people think of John Knox solely in terms of Scotland, and feel therefore that it is for the Scots people only to commemorate him and his work. The answer to that can be put in this way. All who have visited Geneva, and have seen the famous Plaque or Memorial to the great reformers will have noticed that John Knox is included among them. He is in that august company with Calvin and Farel; and that should be sufficient to make us realize not only that John Knox did great and marvellous things in Scotland, but also the international character of his work.

I propose to consider this great man with you in terms of a statement made by Thomas Carlyle—a fellow Scot, of course, but nevertheless a historian of repute who did not say things lightly. He refers to John Knox in his book *Heroes and Hero Worshippers* in these terms. He says, 'He was the chief priest and founder of the faith that became Scotland's, New England's and Oliver Cromwell's—that is of Puritanism.' Carlyle does not actually include England—he should have done—but he includes

New England and Oliver Cromwell. He claims for John Knox that he was the father and founder of a movement that led to remarkable events, not only in the British Isles but far beyond, events which influenced the whole course of history. Is that statement of Carlyle justifiable? Can we substantiate his claim? I propose to demonstrate that Carlyle was in no sense guilty of exaggeration.

❁ ❁ ❁

Before we come to think of Knox in particular as the founder of Puritanism let me give a brief sketch of his life. He was brought up in Roman Catholicism and became a priest. At one time he was known as Sir John Knox. He was brought up in poverty in a poor family, with no aristocratic antecedents, and no one to recommend him. He became the great man he was solely as the result of his own remarkable natural gifts, and still more as the result of his conversion. He was converted in a remarkable manner through the instrumentality of certain of the great first lights of the Reformation in Scotland—George Wishart and others. He underwent a very thorough change, and turned his back, of course, upon Roman Catholicism. He found himself eventually in St Andrews where he began to participate in affairs. At first he did not preach, but later he was forced to do so. As a result of this, when the French captured St Andrews and took a number of prisoners, John Knox found himself working as a slave in a French galley for nearly two years. This was a most exhausting experience in which he suffered, not only the rigours of such a life, but intense cruelty also. This undoubtedly left its mark on the whole of his life, because it undermined his health; and he had a constant struggle against ill health.

Eventually he was able to get out of that situation, and came back to England and Scotland. The situation became too difficult for him in Scotland, so he settled in England. He was appointed as minister and preacher in Berwick-on-Tweed, and he remained there and in Newcastle-upon-Tyne from 1549-51. (There is much dispute as to whether he was born in 1503 or 1504 or about 1513 or 1515. That does not matter. The important point is that he was a man of age when he was converted somewhere in the 1540s, and became a preacher in Berwick and Newcastle.) After that he came down to London, and by this time Edward VI was on the throne. Knox became one of the Court chaplains and Court preachers. He was thus right in the centre of affairs in England, and preached on many occasions before Edward VI and the Court. Edward VI died at the age of 16, and Mary, 'Bloody Mary', came to the throne of England. Knox and a number of others had to escape for their lives. Eventually he went to the Continent and began to study under John Calvin at Geneva; but while there he was called to become joint-pastor of the English refugees who had formed a church at Frankfurt-on-Main. So, very reluctantly, and mainly as the result of the persuasion of Calvin, he went there and ministered to the church. After much trouble and disputation he was turned out from Frankfurt and went to Geneva with a number of other refugees, and there again became the pastor of the English Church from 1556-59. Then in April 1559, after the death of Mary, and when Elizabeth had come to the throne in 1558, he was able to return not only to the British Isles, but to Scotland. He began his great work, his life's work in one sense, in Scotland, in April 1559 and continued there until he died on November 24th, 1572.

There, we have a mere skeleton of an outline of the story of this man. There are many excellent biographies of him. I would commend one of the latest by Jasper Ridley. It well repays careful study and consideration. It is one of the best that has ever been written on him, altogether superior to one that came out some thirty years ago by Lord Eustace Percy.

❁ ❁ ❁

Let us now look at the man himself. No man has ever been more maligned than John Knox. This happened to Calvin also; but it is much more true of Knox. There were elements, perhaps, in his character which called this forth even more than in the case of Calvin; but it is all based upon ignorance and, of course, the malice of Roman Catholics and every other type of Catholic. Inevitably in these days of ecumenicity a man like John Knox becomes the target of vitriolic attacks. The chief interest today is in Mary, Mary Queen of Scots, who is painted up, and idealized, even more than she painted herself!

However, I am not concerned to defend John Knox. He does not need me, or anyone else, to defend him. Let us look at this amazing man. He was of short stature—a fact not without significance! Someone once said that the greatest things in this world had been done by small men and small nations! He was not a handsome man, or in any way distinguished in appearance as judged by modern standards. He was a *strong* man, a rugged man, and from the physical standpoint there was nothing to recommend him except for the fact that there was something that came into his eyes now and again that literally put the fear of God into people. The most striking thing about him was his *ability*. He was not able in the sense that Calvin was able, nor was he a scholar in the sense that Calvin was; but a man can be able without being a scholar. So when I talk about his ability I am thinking in particular of his *sense of discrimination,* of his ability to 'differentiate between things that differ'. This seems to have been one of his most outstanding characteristics, as we shall see.

Another thing about him was his *astounding energy*. Here again is a characteristic of all the great men whom God has used throughout the centuries. How he accomplished all he did can only be explained in terms of the grace of God, but there was something even in the very constitution of the man that accounted for this. I was reading recently that the same thing was true of Daniel Rowland, the great Welsh preacher of the 18th century; and I noticed that his contemporaries always commented on his extraordinary energy. This quality is not only characteristic of great statesmen, and great military leaders and others, it is generally a characteristic of great preachers also. We are reminded of Demosthenes's definition of oratory: it was 'action, action, action'.

Another characteristic of Knox was his *shrewdness*. If ever a man needed shrewdness it was John Knox in the situation in which he found himself. We have been reminded in this Conference of the alliance, or relationship at any rate, between the State and the church, between politics and religion. This was inevitable in those days, and it meant that John Knox had to co-operate with certain politicians in Scotland. One is struck by his extraordinary insight into, and understanding of, the thinking of these men and their duplicity. Several times he saved the Reformation simply because of this shrewdness. Jasper Ridley refers to him as 'a consummate politician'; and so he was, and had to be! These men would have sold the pass many times because they could not see what was really happening. They could not see what the enemy was doing; but John Knox could see it, and with that extraordinary shrewdness of his he was able to save the situation. In many instances he was able to see through the subtleties of the mind and behaviour of Mary, Queen of Scots, and her efforts to nullify his endeavours.

Then I come to his *wisdom*. I am emphasizing these points for this reason, that this man is generally regarded as a bigot, a harsh man, a man who was driven by tremendous conceit and ambition, a man who would brook no disagreement or any kind of opposition. But you cannot read any objective account of him without being amazed at his extraordinary wisdom. He seemed to know exactly how far he could go at every stage, and he never tried to go beyond that point. Some would be urging him onwards, and others would be restraining him; but he always seemed to follow the path of wisdom. For instance, when he was in Berwick he did not openly attack the *Book of Common Prayer* which was officially to be used; he just did not use it. You see the distinction. I emphasize this because I have often had to suggest to some of my younger brethren that this is an important point. You need not always announce and talk about what you are doing; and to act is more important than to talk. Knox did not attack, and call attention to it, and put up a placard and say that he was not going to use the *Prayer Book*; he just did not use it. That indicates moderation and great wisdom.

Knox has sometimes been charged with cowardice because he several times escaped from Scotland—both to England and to the Continent—in times of persecution and great danger. But to me he was being governed by this principle of great wisdom and of shrewdness. He realized that if he stayed in Scotland he would undoubtedly be put to death, as were George Wishart, Patrick Hamilton and others before him. He knew that that would not further the cause; so he escaped. I would justify him in doing so. Sometimes it takes greater courage to escape than to stay and become a martyr.

Then consider his *moderation*. To many people it sounds utterly ridiculous to talk of moderation in the case of John Knox—'that fanatic, bigot and extremist'. But the moderation of the man is almost incredible. Take, for instance, the advice he once gave to the people at Berwick. He was down in London just as Edward VI was coming to the end of his reign, and just before Mary became Queen. He knew that these members of his old church at Berwick would soon be in great difficulties. The *Prayer Book*, though officially introduced, had not been enforced in the diocese of Durham because the then Bishop of Durham, Tunstall, was more Catholic than Protestant, and did not like this Protestant *Prayer Book*; so its use had never been enforced. This had helped Knox, of course, to pay no attention to it; but now he could see that there would be a change, and discipline would be enforced; so he writes to these friends in Berwick and Newcastle and urges moderation upon them.

On what matters should they stand? The great question that was raised at first was, as I shall point out later, the kneeling at the reception of the Communion. Knox's advice to them was, that for the sake of the bigger principles and the greater truths, they should conform on this, and he would excuse their doing so. Now that is the principle of moderation in practice. Take some further examples. When he went to Frankfurt as one of two ministers he found that they had already decided to introduce Calvin's Order of Service. They were agreed about this, and they thought that he would agree immediately, because he was such a great admirer of Calvin. But John Knox was not willing to agree, and for this reason. He said that they must not do that without consulting all the other English refugees in Strassburg, Basle and other places. That is moderation. He would only act in unison with the other brethren. Later he and others drew up an Order of Service of their own, and there was opposition to it. He was more ready than anyone else to accept modifications and various additions to it. Further, as I pointed out in my address last year on the Origins of Puritanism, when you contrast him with Richard Cox, the Anglican who came to Frankfurt and insisted that the church, as he put it, should have 'an English face', and that they must go on using the *Prayer Book* as they had used it in England, Knox did everything conceivable, everything a man could possibly do, to accommodate the opposition and to find agreement. But the intransigence of Richard Cox, and those who followed him, was such as to make agreement totally impossible. This man, who is so often traduced as being intolerant and full of bigotry, stands out in shining contrast as a model of moderation over against those Anglicans who not only opposed him but hounded him out of Frankfurt and made him escape to Geneva.

Let us turn now to his *originality*, which again I want to emphasize. John Knox is sometimes thought of as if he were but a 'gramophone record' of Calvin. That is a complete mistake. Some are perhaps guilty of that charge; but John Knox was an original thinker. He thought for himself, and when his understanding of the Scriptures demanded it, he did not hesitate to disagree with, and to oppose, and to speak against, the views that had been advanced by people such as Tyndale and Calvin himself. He disagreed with Calvin and Tyndale, for instance, about the duty of Christian people with regard to their princes and rulers. He advocated opposition to rulers in certain circumstances, and even revolution, before they came anywhere near—and Calvin in particular—to accepting that teaching. That was a mark of his original thinking. He was not governed by Calvin in this matter, or indeed in anything else, unless he agreed. He thought things out for himself. I am emphasizing this because it is a very important matter. We must not swallow automatically everything we read in books, even from the greatest men. We must examine everything; and Knox did so and, as I say, when he disagreed he was very ready to say so. The same was true of his attitude towards the various ceremonies in the Church of England services. He was ahead of others, as I am going to show, in this matter also, and when he wrote his book *Concerning The Monstrous Regiment of Women,* he was again quite original.

That brings us to his *courage*. It was said of him when he died that he 'never feared the face of man'; and that is true of him. In addition I might add that he never feared the face of woman either! And he had to face two women. One was a very strong woman; and the other, Mary, Queen of Scots, was strong because of her weakness. Weak women can make use of their good looks and their femininity in a way that gives them a kind of strength. Elizabeth I of England lacked the good looks, but she had real strength of character. John Knox had to deal with both of them, and he was not afraid of either. Their great power made no difference to him. His courage is almost incredible. He, in the same way, opposed Cranmer, Ridley, and Peter Martyr. He was never afraid to be alone, and to stand alone. His was the same heroic character that you see in Martin Luther standing in the Diet of Worms and elsewhere.

But consider him as *a preacher*. His great characteristic as a preacher was vehemency. Great preachers are generally vehement; and we should all be vehement. This is not the result of nature only; it arises from the feeling of the power of the gospel. Vehemence is, of course, characterized by power; and John Knox was a most powerful preacher, with the result that he was a most influential preacher.

The effect of his preaching upon Edward VI, to which I shall refer later, was quite remarkable; and that was not only true of Edward VI but of many others also. It is traditional to refer to the effect of his preaching on Mary, Queen of Scots. He could make her weep; not under conviction but in anger. She was afraid of him; she said she was more afraid of his prayers and his preaching than of many regiments of English soldiers. Randolph, a courtier and an ambassador, said this about him and his preaching: 'The voice of one man is able in one hour to put more life into us than five hundred trumpets continually blustering in our ears.' The voice of one man! Many times did one sermon delivered by Knox change the whole situation. When the Lords and others were alarmed, and frightened, and all ready to give in, Knox would go up into a pulpit and preach a sermon; and the entire situation was transformed. One man 'more influential than the blustering of five hundred trumpets in our ears!'

That is what preaching can do, and often has done. This was constantly the case with Knox. Perhaps one of the greatest tributes paid to him in this respect was that done unconsciously by an English ecclesiastic. After Mary had come to the throne of England, a certain Hugh Weston was appointed to be Chairman of a discussion on the Communion Service and other matters which took place in Oxford between Cranmer, Ridley, and others on the one side, and the Roman Catholics on the other side. During the discussion Weston said, 'a runagate Scot'—which meant a refugee Scot—'did take away the adoration and worshipping of Christ in the Sacrament; by whose procurement that heresy was put into the last Common Book, the Prayer Book of 1552. So much prevailed that one man's authority at that time.' Weston was not referring to what had happened in Scotland, but in England. There you have a striking testimony to the power of the preaching of Knox, from the enemy. According to these Roman Catholics John Knox was more responsible for the abolition of the idolatry of 'worshipping the host' in the Communion Service than anyone else. That illustrates the power of his preaching.

We come now to consider John Knox as 'the founder of Puritanism'. Is Carlyle right? Is it true to speak of John Knox as 'high priest and founder of Puritanism'? I touched on this subject last year when dealing with the Origins of Puritanism. I referred to it in passing, and also said that in many ways we could trace back the origins of Puritanism to William Tyndale. I still maintain that; but I also contend that, from the standpoint of an organized body of thought and organisation, what Carlyle claims is justifiable. William Tyndale emphasized certain principles both by his spirit and his action, but they became explicit, I would say, in the case of John Knox. I agree with a writer of the last century, of the name of Lorimer, when he says that the only other candidate for the title of 'founder of Puritanism' was John Hooper, Bishop of Gloucester. I further agree with Lorimer when he says that undoubtedly we have to put Knox before Hooper. They agreed on many things, but there were certain differences between them which will emerge as we proceed.

In what sense, then, is it right to say that Knox was 'the founder of Puritanism'? The first answer is provided by his *originality of thought, his independence*. The Puritan, by definition, is a man of independence, of independent thought. The Puritan is never 'an establishment man'. I mean that not only in terms of 'the establishment of religion', but in terms of any aspect of establishment. This is, to me, a most important point. There are some people who seem to be born 'establishment men'. Whatever sphere of life they are in, they are always on the side of the authorities, and of what has always been done, and conditions as they are. Their great concern is to preserve the past. They are found in the Free Churches as commonly as in the Anglican Communion and other forms of Christianity. They are establishment men; and they always start from that position. Now I maintain that the Puritan, by his very nature and spirit, is never an 'establishment man' because of his independence and originality, his reading of the Scriptures for himself, and his desire to know the truth irrespective of what others may have said or thought.

Secondly, Knox is 'the founder of Puritanism' because he brings out so clearly the guiding principles of Puritanism. That is, first and foremost, *the supreme authority of the Scriptures as the Word of God*. I need not go into this. Roman Catholicism puts the Church, its tradition and its interpretation of Scripture first; and all imperfectly reformed churches have always continued to do the same. But the peculiar characteristic of the Puritan is that he asserts the supreme authority of the Word of God. This was Knox's guiding principle. If a thing could not be justified from the Scriptures he would not have it, and he would not allow it to be introduced.

The second guiding principle was that he believed in *a 'root and branch' reformation*. That is not my term; it is his term, and it became the term of others. In other words, the Puritans were not content with a reformation in doctrine only. This is where Knox, and they, disagreed with the leaders in England. All were agreed about the changes in doctrine. They were all Calvinists and so on, but the *differentia* of Puritanism is that it does not stop at a reformation of doctrine only, but insists that the reformation must be carried through also into the realm of practice. This involves the whole view of the nature of the church. To the Puritan, reformation does not only mean a modification or a slight improvement; it means a 'new formation' of the church—not a mere modification of what has already been—governed by the New Testament and its teaching. That was his second guiding principle.

He desired to get back to the New Testament idea of the church. In conformity with that he said that the church had to be reformed in the matter of her ceremonies, in other words, in her conduct

of worship and in the administration of the Sacraments. He put it in this way. 'In the worship
of God, and especially the administration of the
Sacraments, the rule prescribed in Holy Scripture
is to be observed without addition or diminution',
and 'the church had no right to devise religious
ceremonies and impose significations upon them.'
It was because of this that charges were brought
against him. It was said that he contended 'that
man may neither make nor devise a religion that
is acceptable to God, but man is bound to observe
and to keep the religion that from God is received
without chopping or changing thereof.' He also
taught that 'the sacraments of the New Testament
ought to be administered as they were instituted by
Jesus Christ, and practised by the Apostles. Nothing is to be added to them and nothing to be dimin-
ished from them'. Again, 'the Mass is abominable
idolatry, blasphemous to the death of Christ and a
profanation of the Lord's Supper.' He was charged
with teaching such principles; and he was guilty of
the charge. This was his position.

Such were his guiding principles. But, and this
is most vital in this matter, *he applied his principles*. There is no such thing, it seems to me, as a
theoretical or academic Puritan. There are people

who are interested in Puritanism as an idea; but they are traitors to Puritanism unless they apply its teachings; for application is always the characteristic of the true Puritan. It is all very well to extol the 'Puritan conscience', but if you do not obey your conscience you are denying Puritanism. Hooper agreed with Knox in so many things, but Hooper had a tendency to go back on what he believed. When Hooper was to be ordained as bishop he said that he would not wear the vestments that were customary, and was sent to gaol; but then, afterwards, he gave in and wore the vestments. The point I am establishing is that the true Puritan not only sees these things, and holds these views, he applies them, he acts on them. This is where Knox is so notable, and superior to John Hooper. He stands out in his conscientious application of what he believed to be the New Testament pattern regarding the nature of the church, and the ordinances and the ceremonies, and the exercise of discipline.

Let us now watch him putting these principles into operation. First in Berwick-on-Tweed and Newcastle-upon-Tyne. As we have seen he did not carry out the Edward VI Order of Common Prayer of 1548, neither did he follow the instructions of the *Book of Common Prayer* of 1549. He was helped in this respect by Tunstall. Most other preachers were conforming to it; but not John Knox. He was not governed in his administration of the Sacraments by the decrees of the official body in England under which he was now preaching, nor by the *Prayer Book*.

Secondly—and this is one of the vital points—it was customary to receive the Sacrament in a kneeling posture. This is Anglican practice. John Knox was the first to teach people—and not only to teach them, but to put it into practice—to take the Communion in a sitting position. This is Puritanism in practice. Quite on his own, and by his understanding of the Scriptures, he came to the conclusion that it is wrong to kneel in the reception of the Sacraments. There is very good evidence, I think, for saying that he had already put this view into practice in St Andrews, before he had become a slave in the French galleys; but whether so or not he certainly introduced this practice in Berwick; and it was a great innovation. For centuries under Roman Catholicism the Sacrament had been received in the kneeling position, and this was the custom and the practice in the Reformed Anglican Church. Another innovation, in which he was the leader, was that he substituted bread for the wafer. He no longer used the wafer as had been the custom for centuries in the Roman Church, and as was still the custom in the Anglican Church up to this time. They soon changed this; but Knox was the first to do so; and he did so when he was minister at Berwick-on-Tweed.

With regard to baptism, he refused to baptize the children of people who had been excommunicated. Other ministers did so. He refused private baptism, and he refused to make the sign of the cross in connection with baptism. Those who are familiar with the subsequent history of Puritanism will know that these are all vital matters which became crucial in the Puritan position throughout the years. Knox had introduced these Puritan ideas, in practice, in his ministry both at Berwick and Newcastle.

Knox was taken to London by the Duke of Northumberland and became Court Chaplain, and a popular preacher. We are concerned with his story there only as the founder of Puritanism. A great crisis arose in 1552. A reformed *Prayer Book* had been introduced in 1549, but almost everyone came to agree that it was inadequate, and that there were still too many relics and remnants of Roman Catholicism in it. So it was decided that they must have a new *Prayer Book,* and also new 'Articles of Religion'. They began to prepare them, and by September 1552 a new *Prayer Book* was produced, largely by Thomas Cranmer. They had already also drawn up 45 Articles of Religion—which became the basis of what ultimately became known as the 39 Articles. Here is the crucial point. This new *Prayer Book* had actually been sent to the printers, and was due to come into operation on November 1st, 1552. Copies of this book had been sent to John Knox and the other chaplains and preachers, as a matter of courtesy, assuming, of course, that they would all be in agreement. But, immediately, John Knox saw that it contained something with which he could not agree. He was also unhappy about some of the 45 Articles. Article 38 stated, 'that the second book of Common Prayer was holy, godly and proveable by God's Scriptures, and every rite and ceremony, and at no point repugnant thereto, both as regards the common prayers and the administration of the Sacraments as well as the ordinal'.

This immediately made Knox feel that the position was intolerable. Why? For this extraordinary reason, that in this new *Prayer Book* there was a rubric which commanded the recipient of the Communion to receive it in a kneeling position. Now that had not been stated in the *Prayer Book* of 1549. Why not? For the reason that that had always been the custom and the practice. That had been done under Roman Catholicism, and it had been continued in the Church of England; so it was not mentioned in 1549. Hooper and others had been querying this practice, as well as Knox, and his practice at Berwick and Newcastle had become known. So Cranmer, Ridley, and Peter Martyr and others felt that an instruction should be put into the new *Prayer Book* telling people that they had to receive the sacrament in the kneeling position. Immediately Knox was in trouble. How could he agree to Articles which stated that everything in this new *Prayer Book* was 'holy, godly and proveable by God's Scriptures'? That was not true; it was a lie. So what did he do? Fortunately he had an opportunity of expressing himself. The King (Edward VI) and his Court were at Windsor, and it fell to the lot of John Knox to be the preacher. With his customary courage he preached on this very matter, and did so with such power and effect that he shook the King to his foundations on this matter, and many others with the King. Knox maintained that kneeling was sinful and idolatrous. Remember that he had against him Cranmer, Ridley, and Peter Martyr, and also that the book was already in the hands of the printers, and that in six weeks' time, or less, it was due to be introduced officially on November 1st. Well, this one sermon of Knox caused consternation and led to much activity. Knox, with one or two others, drew up a Memorandum stating their case against kneeling, and pleading that the King and the authorities should not insist upon this kneeling because it was sinful and idolatrous. They presented this Memorandum to the King and Council. After much conferring and arguing, the authorities eventually arrived at a compromise. Knox did not get his wish that this rubric should not be put into the new *Prayer Book*; but he did obtain a vital improvement. He had so convinced the King that the King signed a Declaration which was to be added to the *Prayer Book*. This was a rubric which was to be inserted in order to safeguard against the dangers that arose from kneeling at the reception of the Communion, and especially the possibility of idolatry.

There is little doubt but that this rubric was drawn up by Cranmer. It has the marks of his peculiar genius for compromise. The new *Prayer Book* was already printed but still in the hands of the printers. What could the authorities do? They printed this new rubric, this new declaration on this subject, on a separate sheet of paper, and the King issued a decree that this sheet was to be stuck into the new *Prayer Book*. The few copies of the original printing of that *Prayer Book* that remain still have it.

This is the rubric that John Knox, through the King, had forced Cranmer to produce. It says, 'Although no order can be so perfectly devised, but it may be of some, either for their ignorance and infirmity, or else of malice and obstinacy, misconstrued, depraved, and interpreted in a wrong part: and yet, because brotherly charity willeth that, so much as conveniently may be, offences should be taken away: therefore we, willing to do the same; whereas it is ordained in the Book of Common Prayer, in the administration of the Lord's Supper, that the communicants kneeling should receive the Holy Communion, which thing being well meant for a signification of the humble and grateful acknowledging of the benefits of Christ given unto the worthy receiver, and to avoid the profanation and disorder which about the Holy Communion might else ensue; lest yet the same kneeling might be thought or taken otherwise, we do declare that it is not meant thereby that any adoration is done, or ought to be done, either unto the sacramental bread or wine there bodily received, or unto any real and essential presence there being of Christ's natural flesh and blood. For as concerning the sacramental bread and wine, they remain still in their very natural substances, and therefore may not be adored, for that were idolatry to be abhorred of all faithful Christians; and as concerning the natural body and blood of our Saviour Christ, they are in heaven, and not here; for it is against the truth of Christ's true natural body to be in more places than in one at one time.'

This rubric became known as 'the Black Rubric'. My point is that Knox was the man who was chiefly responsible for its introduction. It was added to the *Prayer Book* as a safeguard against the terrible danger of idolatry. Now that was a purely Puritan action. Queen Elizabeth, when she came to the throne, excluded that Black Rubric from the *Prayer Book,* and it was only restored with slight modification in 1662.

Here is proof positive that this man was the leader of the Puritan party in this explicit manner.

He fought about many other things also, but failed. He tried to change the doctrine in Article 26 on the nature of the sacraments. Knox taught 'that God confers grace independently of the Sacraments, though Sacraments are a sign of grace'. Cranmer, on the other hand, said and printed that 'grace was conferred through the two Sacraments which were not merely a sign or a channel of grace'. There, again, Knox was contending for the Puritan attitude to the Sacraments over against that of Cranmer, Ridley, Peter Martyr and the other typical Anglicans.

Further evidence of Knox's 'puritanism' during this period in London is this. As a result of the trouble over the *Prayer Book,* Knox had become such a prominent man and leader that he was offered the bishopric of Rochester. But he refused it. Hooper accepted the bishopric of Gloucester, but Knox would not accept; and the only explanation of this refusal was his Puritan principles. He never really believed in bishops at all.

Going on to his time in Frankfurt, here, again, a very interesting thing happened. As we have seen, Knox was asked to go from Geneva, where he was studying under Calvin, to be one of the two pastors of the church of the English refugees meeting in Frankfurt. This is surely extraordinary. Here is an English church, a church founded by some great Englishmen who had had to flee for their lives; and they ask this Scotsman to be their minister. Why? Thomas Fuller, a typical Englishman, and not a Puritan, writing in the next century put it thus, 'You may account it incongruous that among so many and able English divines that were then abroad that a Scotsman should be pastor of the English Church at Frankfurt, the most visible and conspicuous beyond the seas; and it was seeing Mr Knox's reputed merit did naturalise him though a foreigner.' That puts it well.

While he was at Frankfurt Knox did something which is typically and characteristically Puritan. He and Whittingham, the main translator of the famous Geneva Bible, drew up an Order of Service to replace that of the *Book of Common Prayer* which they disliked. Modified mainly because of Knox's moderation, this Order had been accepted by the church until Richard Cox and his party arrived. I emphasize the point that John Knox, by drawing up this Order of Service, repudiated the *Book of Common Prayer*. He did not say this openly, once more, until confronted by the militant and ungentlemanly opposition of Richard Cox, whose behaviour can only be described as quite abominable, intransigent and rude—not the last time Puritans have had to suffer in that way at the hands of Anglicans. Cox having adopted this attitude, John Knox was no longer prepared to remain silent. He was prepared not to shout about these things as long as there was a hope of carrying people with him, but when Cox behaved in that scandalous manner, John Knox preached the next day and now stated plainly and clearly his views of the *Book of Common Prayer*. 'At the time appointed for the sermon', he says in his subsequent history of these matters, 'I began to declare what opinion I had . . . (and how) I was driven away from my first opinion.' Here is evidence of a big man: he changes his opinion. It is the small man who never changes his opinion. He went on to explain why he had changed, and to say that he believed that the troubles in England under Mary were the punishment of God upon them for not carrying out Reformation more thoroughly, and especially with regard to this matter of the *Prayer Book*.

There he states plainly and openly his attitude towards the *Prayer Book*. This resulted in his being driven out from Frankfurt; so he went to Geneva. The first attempt at a Puritan church amongst

English people was that in Frankfurt. It was a failure because Cox and his friends resorted to the despicable resort of charging John Knox falsely with high treason against the Emperor, the political judge. This charge was based on certain things he had said, and had printed, in a sermon once preached in Amersham.

The first attempt to form a Puritan church having thus failed in Frankfurt, Knox and his supporters then went to Geneva; and what had failed at Frankfurt became a success in Geneva. Here Knox introduced the Order of Service which had been tried and rejected in Frankfurt. This became the Order of Service in Geneva. It is known as the Geneva Book. This Order in the Geneva Book was not Calvin's Order. Calvin also had his Order; but this was John Knox's primarily, and this was the Order of Service which he subsequently introduced when he returned to Scotland, and which has been used in the Church of Scotland ever since as their official Book of Order.

In Geneva, therefore, we have the first truly Puritan church amongst English people. This provides one of the strongest arguments for asserting with Carlyle that John Knox is the founder of English Puritanism. It was also while at Geneva that he formulated his view with regard to Princes, and the attitude of the Christian towards 'the powers that be'. Here he was ahead of Calvin, and this is again a sign of his true Puritanism. I maintain that one cannot truly understand the revolution that took place here in England in the next century except in the light of this teaching. Here was the first opening of the door that led to that later development.

Also while at Geneva he published his famous treatise *The First Blast of the Trumpet Against the Monstrous Regiment of Women,* the monstrous 'government' by women. John Knox believed that it was contrary to Scripture to have a Queen ruling over the people, and he produced specific statements from the Scriptures to justify his attitude. As the result of this, Knox mortally offended Queen Elizabeth 1. She never forgave him; but he nevertheless prepared a Second Blast which he did not actually publish.

This, again, is not only indicative of his courage and his independence of thought, but, I maintain, it is also a part of his essential Puritanism coming to the surface. I should add, perhaps, to make my story complete, that Knox at times could indulge in a little casuistry. He put forward an explanation of how, in spite of the clear scriptural teaching on this question of a woman monarch, in the peculiar circumstances then prevailing it was allowable for Elizabeth in England and Mary in Scotland to act for the time being as monarchs. That was a bit of casuistry. However, his main position was the one stated in the *First Blast*.

One further fact must be mentioned here. Queen Mary Tudor died and Elizabeth came to the throne in 1558. Knox saw at once new possibilities arising, so he wrote *A Brief Exhortation to England for the Speedy Embracing of Christ's Gospel Heretofore by the Tyranny of Mary Suppressed and Banished*. He sent this from Geneva in 1559; and Elizabeth strongly objected to this Scotsman who was writing to the English to tell them how to conduct their affairs. He wrote in a very strong manner. He was naturally very much concerned about the state of the English Church. He had been pastor amongst English refugees in Frankfurt and Geneva, as well as previously in Berwick and Newcastle. So he addressed this great appeal to them. He reminds them of what had taken place in Mary's time, and again presses upon them the idea that it was God's judgment upon them. He called them to repentance and conversion, and then went on to make an extreme statement which I cannot defend. He was intolerant at this point. He said that 'none ought to be freed from the yoke of the Church discipline, nor permitted to decline from the religion of God.' Further, prince, king or emperor who should try to destroy God's true religion and introduce idolatry should 'be adjudged to death according to God's commandment'. Let me say this in mitigation. Knox never was the means or the cause of anyone being put to death. He stated that in principle, but he never carried it out himself in practice. That was one of those extreme statements which it is difficult to defend.

In this exhortation to England, this programme of ecclesiastical and educational reform, he advocated the setting up of schools where people could be taught and instructed in the Scriptures. This was a programme for ecclesiastical and educational reform and, I would claim, is the first printed outline of reform ever published by the Puritan party of the national church. This is a weighty document. It is the first printed statement of Puritan principles with regard to the church and her management. In it Knox shows his dislike of bishops and suggests as a practical reform that every bishopric be divided into ten parts, that where there had been one Lord Bishop there should be ten preaching men, that these men should be preaching regularly, and that these great dioceses and these princes of the church should be abolished. Big dioceses should be reduced to ten manageable bodies, and godly, learned men should be instructed to preach and to give instruction to the people in every city and town. In addition he advocated the setting up of schools. Then he returned to Scotland and remained there for the rest of his life. But this did not bring to an end his connection with English Puritanism. He began to hear that the people who had followed him, in other words the true Puritans, were being persecuted by the bishops, some of whom were men who had been members of the congregation in Frankfurt or in Geneva. So he wrote a letter from Scotland to the bishops in England remonstrating with them, and pleading with them not to persecute the Puritans. He writes as a true Puritan to those other Puritans who were beginning to compromise in England, and shows clearly his attitude to vestments, surplices, *etc.,* which he describes as 'Romish rags'. There speaks the true Puritan.

He also wrote a letter to the sufferers in England in 1567. This letter causes perplexity to some because he seems to discourage them. Some of these suffering Puritans wrote to him and pleaded with him to come out plainly on their side. He had already done so, in a sense, in his letter to the bishops; but he wrote back to these people and exhorted them not to break or to trouble the common order 'thought meet to be kept for unity and peace for a time'. In other words, he told them not to secede, not to be separatists. He was opposed to separation; but let me emphasize the fact that he introduced the term 'for a time'. Knox is often misunderstood at this point. People argue that he did not believe in separation, and that he was really on the side of the 'conforming Puritans'. That was not the case. This letter is but another example and illustration of his extraordinary spirit of discrimination. Knox always seemed to understand that the position of England was a peculiar one; and he was surely right. This Scotsman had the sense and the understanding and the ability to see that the Englishman is *sui generis*. The Englishman—and you cannot ignore these things—has a genius for compromise. He has a hatred of definitions and precise statements. He still boasts of the fact that when he had an Empire it did not have a written Constitution! He glories in the fact that he has always 'muddled through'. Knox always recognized this, so when he was in London he was prepared to do things which he had not done in Berwick and Newcastle, and which he most certainly did not, and would not, do in Frankfurt and Geneva, and when he went back to Scotland. But when he writes to these people in England he knows the position is different; and so, appearing to contradict himself, he advises them to tolerate certain things, and to conform. He argues that, while the authorities are still preaching the truth in general, they should not break with them over this particular matter.

Note that he emphasizes 'for a time'. He felt that there was still hope that the force of truth would soon prevail, and that all would come to see that they should get rid of the 'Romish rags' and all the other relics of Romanism. Of course, that did not come to pass; and Knox himself died in 1572. So what appears to be inconsistency is, rather, a mark of wisdom and understanding.

His influence upon Puritanism in England did not end there. It went on even after his death. Knox wrote a *History of the Reformation in Scotland,* and it is very interesting to notice that that *History* was first published, not in Scotland, but in England by the English Puritans in 1587. Not only so, John Field, a leading Puritan who printed another treatise by John Knox, in introducing that treatise paid him a most glowing tribute, referring to him as 'so worthy and notable an instrument of God' and describing the treatise as 'a seal of his godly and wonderful labours, carrying in the forehead thereof of what an heroical and bold spirit he was.'

Knox's influence even continued into the next century. John Milton, in writing a treatise justifying the putting to death of Charles I, leaned heavily upon John Knox. That is why I put such emphasis upon his perspicacity, and his understanding of the Scriptures, in this matter of not only opposing rulers at times, but even, if necessary, of putting them to death. The fact that John Milton recognized this is surely a powerful proof of the fact that Knox is the founder of Puritanism. In 1683, when Charles II was beginning to show openly that he was a Roman Catholic, at the command of the authorities the works of John Knox were burned in public in Oxford, and a prohibition was issued that his works should not be read. 1683, and Knox died in 1572! His influence continued and was feared. He is indeed the founder of English Puritanism as well as of that of Scotland.

Consider the case of the Pilgrim Fathers. Knox is behind their whole attitude towards the State and the rulers; and so he is, as Thomas Carlyle claims, the founder of American Puritanism in exactly the same way. Indeed, I would argue that he is in many ways the father of the American War of Independence which came to a triumphant conclusion from the standpoint of the colonists in 1776. He was the one who opened the door to all this.

What do we make of this man? He was a man for his age; a man for his times. Special men are needed for special times; and God always produces such men. A mild man would have been useless in the Scotland of the 16th century, and in many other parts of this country. A strong man was needed, a stern man, a courageous man; and such a man was John Knox. Martin Luther was of the same mould. God uses different types of men, and gives them different personalities. Different men are needed at different times. In those times an heroic, rugged character was needed; and God produced the man.

Lest any should continue thinking that he was a hard man, I close by referring to his extraordinary *humility*. 'Humility in John Knox?' says someone. He was a most humble man. The fact that a man stands boldly for the Truth, and does not yield, does not mean that he is not humble. He is not standing for himself, he is standing for the Truth. I can prove that John Knox was a very much humbler man than many in the ministry today. He was in St Andrews after his conversion, and was invited to preach; but he refused. He would not preach, alleging, and these are his words, 'that he would not run where God had not called him', meaning that he would do nothing without a sense of lawful vocation. Knox would not preach without being absolutely certain of his call. A chaplain called John Rough turned to Knox on a certain day, and called on him to preach and not to refuse the burden. He asked the congregation to show that they had instructed him to call upon Knox, and the congregation called out that this was so. Here was a whole congregation calling upon Knox to preach. What was his response? 'At this Knox burst into tears and withdrew to his room.' He remained in a state of deep depression and anxiety until the day of his first sermon came. 'Everyone could see how gloomy he was, for he never smiled, avoided company as much as possible, and spent all his time by himself.'

What a contrast to men who are always ready to run up pulpit steps to preach! This is true humility, and also the Puritan spirit. It is 'the fear of the Lord', the dread of standing between God and man, and proclaiming 'the unsearchable riches of Christ'. The Puritan never believes that every man who is converted is thereby called to preach, or that he can run whenever he likes at his own calling. He wants to know for certain that he is called, because he is so deeply conscious of the sacredness of the task. Like Paul the Apostle he does this 'in weakness, and in fear, and in much trembling'.

Knox is generally regarded as being an arrogant man, and one who was rude in the presence of Mary, Queen of Scots. But that is all based on the fallacy of what makes a man a 'ladies' man'. It is based also on a misunderstanding of true womanhood, and what a true woman really likes. The general idea of a 'ladies' man' is one of a 'society fop'. But that is not a 'ladies' man', and a woman worthy of the name has no regard for a fop. A true woman likes a strong man; and as you read the life of this man you find that many of his correspondents were women. This stern reformer, this man who battled with Lords and Princes, and who would stand up to all authorities, spent much of his time in going into the details of what Charles Lamb once described as 'the mumps and measles of the soul'. These women had their personal problems and difficulties, their 'cases of conscience'; and he always had time to write to them. He often wrote at great length, with great tenderness. When he was in Geneva two women took a dangerous journey over land and sea in order to be near him and to partake of his ministry. His correspondence with his mother-in-law, Mrs Bowes, and also Mrs Ann Lock, over many years, is proof positive that this man had a most tender spirit when you really got to know him, and when he knew he was dealing with a true and honest and genuine soul. That is another sign of his humility. A further sign was this. When he went back to Scotland he appointed Superintendents in the church—not bishops. He did that because it was essential at the time. It was only a temporary expedient, and it was dropped later; but the interesting point is that he never became a Superintendent himself. He was only a preacher to the end. He did not appoint himself as a Superintendent, still less as an Arch-superintendent. All these things are signs not only of his humility, but also of his essential Puritan spirit.

So let us take farewell of this noble, rugged, and yet tender, and even lovable spirit, as he came to leave this world, and to receive his eternal reward.

This is the account given by his daughter. 'At about mid-day, he asked his wife to read aloud the 15th chapter of the First Epistle to the Corinthians, and said that he commended his soul, spirit and body to God, ticking off his soul, spirit, and body on three of his fingers. At about 5 p.m. he said, "Go and read where I cast my first anchor", and his wife read to him the 17th chapter of John's Gospel. When evening prayers were read about 10 p.m. his physician asked him if he heard the prayers. Knox replied, "I would to God that ye and all men heard them as I have heard them; and I praise God of that heavenly sound."' 'Now it is come,' he shortly added. Those were his last words, and there can be no doubt that as he crossed, the heavenly trumpets sounded on the other side as this great warrior of God entered in, and received his eternal 'crown of glory'.

JOHN KNOX
AND 'THE BATTLE'

IAIN H. MURRAY

'Now, O Lord, thou hast revealed thyself and thy beloved Son Jesus Christ, clearly to the world again, by the true preaching of his blessed evangel, which also of thy mercy is offered unto us within this realm of Scotland . . . Give unto us, O Lord, that presently are assembled in thy Name, such abundance of thy Holy Spirit, that we may see those things that shall be expedient for the advancement of thy glory, in the midst of this perverse and stubborn generation. Give us grace, O Lord, that universally among ourselves, we may agree in the unity of true doctrine. Bless thou so our weak labours, that the fruits of the same may redound to the praise of thy holy Name, to the profit of this present generation, and to the posterity to come, through Jesus Christ; to whom, with thee and the Holy Ghost, be all honour and praise, now and ever. So be it.'

John Knox remains one of the most controversial figures in history. Even his fellow countrymen are divided over him. Many have asserted that he was 'the greatest of Scotsmen',[1] but the more modern view is that of Dr Charles Warr who wrote, 'Of Christian virtues he had but few.'[2] Connected with this difference is a fundamental disagreement over the state of Scotland in the sixteenth century. History is not only about facts, it is about how they are to be interpreted. Let us begin with some facts. On the last day of February 1528, a young man of twenty-four years was executed by being burned alive at St Andrews. He was Patrick Hamilton, and over the next thirty years some twenty men and a woman were to endure a similar death—sometimes singly, as in Glasgow and Cupar; sometimes

---

[1] James Stalker, *His Ideas and Ideals* (London: Hodder and Stoughton, 1904), p. v. 'For the mass of his countrymen, Knox is the greatest person their country has produced.' P. Hume Brown, *John Knox, A Biography* (London: Black, 1895), vol. 2, p. 298.

[2] Charles L. Warr, *The Presbyterian Tradition* (London: Maclehose, 1933), p. 303.

in groups, two and then another four in Edinburgh in the 1530s; and finally, in 1558, a man of more than eighty years of age, Walter Milne (sometimes called Mill), endured the last such fire in St Andrews.[3]

The popular interpretation of these facts is that they only illustrate the kind of behaviour that is caused by religious bigotry and superstition. It was part of a dark age that people could be put to death merely for matters of opinion. But there is a very different explanation, and it is to be found in the book which was prohibited reading in the Scotland of the 1530s. This was William Tyndale's translation of the New Testament and there, in the book of the Revelation, it speaks of 'witnesses' being put to death, and shows that the sufferings of the Christian church between Christ's first and second advents are not due, in the first instance, to human folly but to demonic evil. Certainly the Devil uses men, and the way he does so is set down in that same Scripture. We read in Revelation chapter 13 of Satan's purpose being expressed through two 'beasts': the one nations and their governments,

[3] For summary, see David Hay Fleming, *The Reformation in Scotland* (London: Hodder and Stoughton, 1910), pp. 194–200.

the other false religion—religion that *looks like* a lamb but speaks lies as a dragon (*Rev.* 13:11). By such passages God gave to the martyrs a true understanding of their sufferings.

Patrick Hamilton and those who followed him were put to death by the church of their day. It was a church abundant in possessions, revenues, and men. In a country where the population was only around 800,000, priests numbered perhaps as many as 3,000. Amid a poor population the church owned the finest buildings in the land. But it was a church far gone in moral and intellectual decay. While celibacy was professed by the clergy, living with concubines was commonplace among them. Archbishop David Beaton was known to have eight illegitimate children, and the Bishop of Moray had ten. The sons of such liaisons were given lucrative church positions and for the daughters there was the hope of marriage among the nobility. When in 1549, too late in the day, the church began to think of reform, the crass ignorance that abounded in the religious orders was openly admitted. Some priests, it appeared, could scarcely say the alphabet. Preaching from the Bible had long since disappeared, and anyone doing so was instantly suspected of being a Protestant. One such suspect, a monk, was examined by the Bishop of Dunkeld who said that he had no objection to preaching provided it stuck to 'any good gospel or any good epistle that setteth forth the liberty of the Holy Church'. The prisoner shrewdly replied that he did not know how to distinguish in the Bible between good gospels and epistles and evil, and asked the bishop to enlighten him. The bishop, lost for an answer, could only exclaim, 'Thank God, I never knew what the Old and New Testament was, and I will to know nothing but my breviary and my pontifical.'[4]

Before the middle of the sixteenth century in Scotland the need for reformation was recognized on all hands; what was not recognized was that wrong living was the consequence of wrong believing. The church could not have grown so fat and bloated had it not been for the money raised from her teaching on the sacraments, purgatory, indulgences and such like. What made the Protestant witnesses so obnoxious to the clergy was the recognition that if their message prevailed then the absolute authority of the church over the souls of men and women would be at an end. This is clear enough in the charges laid against the martyrs.

[4] J. H. Merle d'Aubigné, *History of the Reformation in Europe*, vol. 6 (London: Longmans, 1875), p. 123.

Patrick Hamilton was condemned for affirming that sacraments cannot save. The first charge against him at his trial was that he said 'The corruption of sin remains in a child after baptism.' Another charge was his statement that 'A man is not justified by works, but by faith alone.'[5] His opponents saw that the evangelicals were moving the whole basis of salvation from the church to Christ. 'Christ', said Hamilton, 'bare our sins on his back and bought us with his blood.'[6]

The modern idea is that the religious division of the sixteenth century was little more than a difference over terminology, and that both sides have equal entitlement to be regarded as Christian. To say that is to remain ignorant of 'the power of darkness' which prevailed in Scotland before the Reformation. The gospel itself was not known. It was because the Protestant martyrs knew from what they had been delivered that they did not regard the difference with their persecutors as a matter of opinion. The issue was the way of salvation. Speaking of the counsellors of the Queen Regent in 1560, Knox was to say, 'These ignorant Papists that were

[5] A. F. Mitchell, *The Scottish Reformation* (Edinburgh: Blackwood, 1900), p. 31.

[6] d'Aubigné, *History*, vol. 6, p. 50.

JOHN KNOX AND THE REFORMATION

about her understood nothing of the Mystery of our Redemption.'⁷

To recognize this is to see that the Reformation was no mere disagreement between two groups of men. With the Bible open before them, the reformers knew that there was an enemy whose great aim was to silence the voice of the gospel. The most frequently used word in John Knox's vocabulary was undoubtedly the word 'battle'; and the battle, as he knew it, was 'not against flesh and blood, but against principalities, against powers, against the rulers of the darkness of this world' (*Eph.* 6:12).

The Early Years, 1514–59

John Knox was born about the year 1514,⁸ and into a family which knew something of conflicts of a different kind. He was a native of Haddington

---

⁷ John Knox, *History of the Reformation in Scotland*, ed. C. J. Guthrie (repr., Edinburgh: Banner of Truth, 1982) p. 222. Hereafter quoted as Guthrie, *Knox*.

⁸ In the seventeenth century a manuscript statement of his age at death was given as '57', but it was misread as '67', thus making the date of his birth ten years earlier than it was. This mistake was followed by all writers until Hay Fleming identified it in 1904. That 57 was the correct age of Knox at death is confirmed by a letter from Peter Young to Beza in November 1579. See P. Hume Brown, *John Knox, A Biography,* vol. 2 (London: 1895), pp. 322–3.

in East Lothian. His father and grandfathers had served under the standards of the Hepburns, Earls of Bothwell, and it may be that under those standards one or more of them had died at Flodden in 1513. Few there were in Scotland in those days who had not been in warfare of one kind or another. Life was cheap and times were brutal. Sudden death by various means was not uncommon. We read, for instance, of an English soldier who raided a Scots house for provisions and, while he was bent double, peering into a barrel of meal, a female took him by the ankles so that he fell in head-first and there she put an end to him.

Knox was about fourteen years old when Patrick Hamilton died at St Andrews. It cannot have been long after that event that he became a student in that old university town; yet the burning of Hamilton evidently did not change his religion, for one of the first definite facts we know about Knox is that he was ordained to the priesthood in 1536. He then became a church lawyer, an 'apostolic notary', and there is evidence that in that office he was occupied in East Lothian between 1540 and 1543. At what time it 'pleased God to call me from the puddle of Papistry',[9] he does not tell us. We know that in

---

[9] *Works of John Knox,* ed. David Laing, vol. 3 (Edinburgh,

1542–43 a change in government allowed a temporary toleration for Protestants and that a friar by the name of Thomas Guylliame preached the gospel in East Lothian and Edinburgh: 'He was the first man', writes David Calderwood, 'from whom Mr Knox received any taste of the truth.'[10]

If Knox did not become a Christian until about 1543, we can be sure that the next three years were spent in hard study of the Scriptures, for when he first emerges into clear view in 1546–7 it is as a man already able to use the Word of God with telling effect. He was then about thirty-two years of age and no longer earning his living from the church but from the tuition of pupils. We learn this from his most important book, his *History of the Reformation in Scotland*. This work was not written as an autobiography and his name first enters the pages almost incidentally in connection with the ministry of George Wishart, by whose preaching, he says, 'God wrought so wonderfully' at this time.

When Wishart came to East Lothian to preach in the winter of 1545–6 Knox 'waited upon him carefully'.

1895), p. 439. Hereafter, Laing, *Knox*.

[10] David Calderwood, *History of the Kirk of Scotland*, ed. Thomas Thomson (Edinburgh: Wodrow Soc., 1842), vol. 1, p. 156.

This function included guarding the reformer with a two-handed sword against would-be assassins. The companionship of Wishart and Knox ended suddenly at the command of the older man who sensed that his work was done and wanted the life of Knox preserved for another day. 'Return to your pupils', he told Knox, 'and God bless you. One is sufficient for one sacrifice.' That same day a few hours later, at midnight, Wishart was taken, and later burned by Cardinal Beaton, outside Beaton's castle in St Andrews, on March 1, 1546. Among his last words were these:

> I beseech thee, Father of heaven! To forgive them that have of any ignorance or else have of any evil mind forged any lies upon me: I forgive them with all my heart. I beseech Christ to forgive them that have condemned me to death this day ignorantly.[11]

Not all professing Protestants were of Wishart's spirit, and two months later David Beaton was also dead, murdered by intruders in his own stronghold. The death of Beaton was one of the first actions by which revolution became confused with Reformation. A connection between the two things would later give the opponents of the gospel excuse to

[11] d'Aubigné, *History*, vol. 6, p. 244.

attribute the progress of evangelical Christianity to physical force, but as Merle d'Aubigné has observed of the murder of Beaton: 'Such things are more likely to ruin a cause than to save it. The Christian life and death of Wishart contributed far more powerfully than the death of Beaton to the advancement of the kingdom of God.'[12]

After the death of Beaton the castle of St Andrews became a refuge for a mixed multitude of whom the majority were Protestants. Finding himself increasingly in danger of the same treatment as Wishart suffered, Knox, with three pupils, also went there at Easter, 1547. Here his real life-work began. Others in the castle, hearing the way he taught his pupils, compelled him to take up the public teaching of the Scriptures. This he did from the Gospel of John, but it was not for long. In August of that same year the castle fell before the attack of eighteen French galleons, and the 120 defenders, Knox among them, went as prisoners to France.

What French forces were doing in Scotland in 1547 requires some explanation. It all had to do with royal marriages, which were so often arranged with political aims in view. At the beginning of the sixteenth century, Scotland and England, traditional

[12] *Ibid.*, p. 257.

enemies, were linked by the marriage of Margaret Tudor (sister of Henry VIII of England) to James IV of Scotland. But good relations with England soon broke down, especially after the son of James IV—James V—married the French noblewoman, Mary of Guise. They had a daughter, Mary, Queen of Scots, who succeeded to the Scottish throne when she was only one week old. King Henry VIII saw the opportunity of uniting the two nations by arranging a marriage between her and his son Edward but, instead, the French connection prevailed and the infant Mary was sent to France by her mother where she remained for thirteen years for education in the dissolute French court.

From 1545, Mary of Guise proceeded to govern Scotland as Regent and to treat it as though it were a part of France. In Knox's words, 'France began to thirst to have the regiment of Scotland in their own hands.'[13] The outcome of these national relationships was to have a close

[13] Knox, *History of the Reformation in Scotland,* in Laing, *Knox,* vol. 1, p. 233. There are three versions of Knox's *History.* Guthrie, *Knox,* is a popular abridgement. Laing is complete. William Croft Dickinson produced a fine edition, *John Knox's History of the Reformation in Scotland* (London: Nelson, 1949), with the spelling of the Laing text modernized throughout.

bearing on the recovery of the gospel, for while the Protestant cause was favoured in England, from the throne of France it had only resolute opposition.

A vital part of Knox's preparation for future usefulness lay in his experience of both France and England after his capture in 1547. He can have seen comparatively little of France itself for he tells us that, following his capture, nineteen months were spent as a slave in a French galley. Galleys commonly had about fifty rowers on ten-foot-long benches, four feet apart, and with six men on each bench responsible for an oar fifty feet long (thirteen feet inside the boat and thirty-seven outside). To these benches the slaves were chained as the sea washed freely across the low deck.[14] Then, apparently at English intervention, Knox was released and reached England in 1549. These were the days of the young Edward VI, and his Protestant government appointed the Scot to preach in the wild northern borders, first at Berwick, then at Newcastle, and finally he was brought to London where he was a chaplain to the Duke of Northumberland.

[14] I am assuming that French galleys changed little between this date and the end of the seventeenth century.

These brighter years in England ended in 1553 when Mary Tudor succeeded her half-brother and restored the Roman faith. Leading Protestants were arrested, but for some months Knox went on preaching, only crossing the English Channel to safety at the beginning of March 1554. Before his departure from England, he tried to get back to Berwick. He had a special reason to go there.

One of the people who had come under the power of the gospel during his Berwick ministry was Elizabeth Bowes, who lived in the border fortress of Norham Castle, seven miles from Berwick, where her husband, Richard, was in command. The Bowes family was one of the most influential in the north, and it was their teenage daughter, Marjory, who became the betrothed wife of Knox about 1552–3.

He had left her in the north for greater safety and could not get back to her before he was compelled to fly for his life. His flight troubled him:

> Albeit that I have in the beginning of this battle appeared to play the faint-hearted and feeble soldier (the cause I remit to God), yet my prayer is, that I may be restored to the battle again.

For the next few years Knox was in several places, including Dieppe, Frankfurt, and Geneva. While a galley slave, God had given him the conviction that he would preach in St Andrews again before he died, but this hope was not fulfilled during a short and hazardous visit to his homeland in 1556. He returned to Europe, and the English congregation at Geneva became his home and congregation.

These twelve hard years of exile from Scotland ended in 1559. Mary Tudor was dead, the Protestant faith was publicly restored in England, and the preparation that Knox needed for 'the battle' in Scotland was now complete.

The Preparation of the Leader

Of the lessons he had learned during that period there are three which stand out.

1. *Knox became a man of prayer*. Prayer as 'an earnest and familiar talking with God', is not natural to us. It is by sanctified trouble and by the recognition of our own helplessness that we learn to pray. 'Out of weakness made strong' is the biblical principle. 'Call upon me in the day of trouble' became a promise of special significance to Knox. His first writing when the Marian persecution broke in England in 1554, was on *What True Prayer Is, How We Should Pray, and For What We Should Pray*.[15] In another place he says that the Apostle

[15] Laing, *Knox*, vol. 3, p. 83.

Peter, as he sought to cross the water to Jesus, was allowed to sink because there was in him too much 'presumption and vain trust in his own strength'. 'Unless it had been corrected and partly removed', he comments, Peter 'had never been apt or meet to feed Christ's flock.'[16] This was surely what Knox himself was being taught. He says that he wrote so much on prayer because,

> I know how hard is the battle between the spirit and the flesh, under the heavy cross of affliction, where no worldly defence but present death does appear. I know the grudging and murmuring complaints of the flesh . . . calling all his promises in doubt, and being ready every hour utterly to fall from God. Against which rests only faith, provoking us to call earnestly and pray for assistance of God's Spirit; wherein, if we continue, our most desperate calamities shall be turned to gladness, and to a prosperous end. To thee alone, O Lord, be praise, for with experience I write this and speak.[17]

Whatever men thought of Knox, none could deny that he was a man of prayer. It is said that even the master of the French galley in which he

[16] *Ibid.*, vol. 3, p. 316.
[17] *Ibid.*, vol. 3, p. 102.

was a slave, during a severe storm, once called on him to pray for their survival.[18] His future work would not have been possible had he not learned dependence on God.

2. Knox's long exile made him an *international Christian*. Had he remained always in Scotland he might have remained as parochial as some of his contemporaries. It was in God's design that he spent most of his time away from home among the English. These were the people against whom his forefathers had fought, but in Christ the old enmity was gone. He was ahead of his time in foreseeing a common Protestant faith binding the two nations together, and that hope became central to his life. 'Grant, O Lord', he prayed, 'we never enter into hostility against the realm and nation of England.'[19] He married an English wife, and came to speak English rather than his native Scots. On his brief visit to Scotland in 1556, report spread of a preacher having appeared in Ayrshire. The preacher was an Englishman, some said, going by his accent. 'Nay, no Englishman', a cleric discerned, 'but it is Knox, that knave.'[20]

---

[18] This was recorded by two contemporary Catholic writers, quoted in Guthrie, *Knox*, p. 96n.

[19] *The Liturgy of John Knox* (Glasgow: Morison, 1886), p. 125.

[20] Laing, *Knox*, vol. 4, p. 439.

3. It was during Knox's exile, and especially in the final years in Geneva, that *the master-principles which governed his thought on Reformation came to maturity*. In outline, they may be stated as follows:

(i.) We exist for God's glory; therefore zeal for the honour of God is the essence of true piety; conversely, to despise God, to offend his majesty, is the darkest form of human depravity. The indignation Knox felt against Roman Catholicism sprang from this source. He saw it as a system bound up with giving to men and to idols that which belongs to God alone. The mass is not a mere mistake about the nature of the sacrament; in its insistence that bread becomes Christ, it is idolatry.

(ii.) Christians are bound to a universal obedience to the Word of God, no matter what the cost, no matter what the consequences. More particularly, nothing is lawful in the church unless it is to be found in Scripture. To quote the reformer's later words to Queen Elizabeth: 'Whatsoever he approves (by his eternal Word), that shall be approved, and what he damneth, shall be condemned, though all men in the earth should hazard the justification of the same.'[21]

[21] *Ibid.,* vol. 6, p. 49.

(iii.) The true church is to be distinguished from the false church in this manner: the true has Christ as its living head, it hears his voice, it follows him, and a stranger it will not follow. This church, further, is to be kept separate from the world by the faithful exercise of discipline in order that reproach is not brought upon God by the character of its members, so that the good is not affected by the evil, and so that those corrected may be recovered.[22]

Success and Conflict, 1559–72

Knox finally returned to Scotland on May 2, 1559. That very day, at the monastery of the Black Friars in Edinburgh, the Roman bishops and priests were met to discuss reformation in the church. The decisions they took included the following:

> That none should enjoy benefice ecclesiastical except he be a priest; that if any priest was found in open adultery, for the first fault he should lose a third of his benefice; and none should put his own son in his benefice.

Elsewhere in Scotland a very different kind of reformation was underway, and in this reformation there were two differing elements at work.

[22] *Ibid.*, vol. 4, p. 204.

The first was the spiritual movement which had gone on secretly in the years of persecution. Despite the prohibition of Tyndale's New Testament, it was read. 'Their tyranny notwithstanding', wrote Knox, 'the knowledge of God did wondrously increase within this realm, partly by reading, partly by brotherly conference, which in those dangerous days was used to the comfort of many.'[23] In this way communities of believers came into existence that met in homes or in the fields as hidden congregations or 'privy kirks'. How many such people there were who, at the risk of their lives, abandoned the Roman Catholic faith, it is impossible to know, but judging by the alarm that they caused to the authorities they were not inconsiderable in some parts. Rewards were offered to any who informed on the secret conventicles. In 1554 Archbishop Hamilton informed the Pope how 'a great part of the diocese of Glasgow' was 'infected with heresies'. John Leslie, a Catholic writer of the period, noted how the Protestant preaching went on 'in chimney nooks, secret holes and such private places, to trouble the whole country'.[24] It was the

---

[23] *Ibid.*, vol. 1, p. 61.

[24] This and the preceding quotation I owe to James Kirk's chapter on 'The "Privy Kirks" and Their Antecedents: The

existence of these 'privy kirks' which explains how parish churches could be so readily established once liberty was granted.

The other element in the Scottish Reformation that led to liberty was the military and the revolutionary. Whether it is justified to speak in terms of 'revolution' has been debated at length—is it revolution for a people to act against the oppression of an absolute monarchy? In any case, the Scots nobility (often at odds with the throne) had a legitimate title to a share in the government, and there was only a regent and no monarch in Scotland until 1561 when Mary, Queen of Scots returned. Before Knox's return in 1559 a number of the Scottish nobility and landowners, assisted by what he calls 'the gentlemen of the west' (lairds in the south-west of Scotland), had joined together in self-defence against the persecution of 'professors of the Evangel', and in patriotic opposition to the French domination.

These men, 'the Lords of the Congregation' (*i.e.,* of the evangelicals), now became the leaders of an armed struggle against Mary of Guise. Thus

---

Hidden Face of Scottish Protestantism', in his book *Patterns of Reform: Continuity and Change in the Reformation Kirk* (Edinburgh: T. & T. Clark, 1989).

two armies faced each other, one of French and Scots supporting the established power and the Catholic cause, and the other of Scots led by some of their own aristocracy who wanted change. The spiritual leadership of the Lords of the Congregation was now given to Knox, who also employed all his English connections to secure aid from that quarter, including money to maintain the payment of their soldiers in the field. Throughout 1559 the outcome remained highly uncertain. In November it seemed that the cause of the Protestant forces was lost as the French took Edinburgh. The Lords of the Congregation retreated in disarray to Stirling and it was left to Knox to rally their demoralized army by his preaching.

Soon after this, the appeals to England for help bore fruit and in 1560 military support came. Then a sight new for Scotland was that of the old enemies of so many battles standing side by side against the French. It was this combination of the spiritual and the para-military that now changed the course of history. Mary of Guise died, and by the Treaty of Edinburgh the French forces agreed to leave Scotland.

The Protestant cause had triumphed, and at the meeting of the Scots Parliament in 1560 a

Confession of Faith, drawn up by Knox and a few colleagues, was ratified. Roman Catholic teaching and practice was henceforth forbidden. The 'privy kirks' now replaced the old parish churches and overnight the congregation of those who professed the evangel became the new national church.

To all appearances this was a sweeping victory, yet the reality was somewhat different. Instead of finding that his 'battle' was over, Knox faced another twelve years of conflict from which only death would deliver him. Mary, Queen of Scots returned to Scotland as sovereign in 1561 and took up residence in the Palace of Holyrood in Edinburgh. She was well trained in the arts of diplomacy and deception. Almost immediately the coalition which had supported Knox began to falter. Some of the leading nobles who had professed Protestantism now defended the right of the Queen to have the Mass and the practice of her religion within her own palaces. Speaking of this new disappointment, Knox wrote to Ann Lock, a friend in London, on October 2, 1561:

> The permission of that odious idol, the Mass, by such as have professed themselves enemies to the same, does hourly threaten a sudden plague. I thirst to change this earthly tabernacle,

before that my wretched heart should be assaulted with such new dolours[25] . . . If you, or any other think that I, or any other preacher within this realm, may amend such enormities, you are deceived; for we have discharged our consciences, but remedy there appears none . . . Our nobility (I write with dolour of heart) begin to find ease good service for God . . . I have finished in open preaching the Gospel of Saint John, saving only one chapter. Oft have I craved the miseries of my days to end with the same.[26]

The bright prospects of 1560 were thus already looking dim. For the next six years Knox was to be in continual conflict with Queen Mary and her supporters. Lord Eustace Percy, in his popular biography of Knox, wrote of the years 1562–5:

Holyrood may well celebrate this prosperous weather with masque and music and dancing. But Knox is in a very different mood. Everywhere Calvin's Reformation hangs on the verge of defeat. All is wrong in Scotland, churches without ministers, ministers without stipends, 'avarice, oppression of the poor, excess, riotous cheer'.[27]

[25] 'Dolour'= pain, grief, sorrow.
[26] Laing, *Knox*, vol. 6, p. 130.
[27] Lord Eustace Percy, *John Knox* (London: Hodder and

Knox and his helpers had drawn up a Book of Discipline for the Reformed Church in 1560, but it was an ominous portent of the future that Parliament refused to ratify it. A church which ceased to be a sanctuary for the worldly remained a vision for the future and the vision was not forwarded by too many priests who now became nominal Protestants. A historian of the Scottish Reformation has written:

> The proposal made in 1560 to exclude the existing clergy from the ministry was proved an idle threat . . . it can be said with some confidence that well over 50 per cent of the staff of the Reformed church was recruited from men who had been in orders before the Reformation.[28]

Some of them, indeed, had known a true change of heart; others were rather of the class of those who, to use the words of Knox, made 'flesh and blood their God'.[29]

Stoughton, n.d. [1934]), p. 385. It is true there was a brighter side than this description conveys. It seems that the reformers were able to fill about a quarter of the parish churches with ministers. See James Kirk, *Patterns of Reform*, p. 130.

[28] Gordon Donaldson, *The Scottish Reformation* (Cambridge: University Press, 1960), p. 85.

[29] Spiritual and other influences were almost chaotically

But for the resolution and courage of Knox the whole Reformation might have failed. In vain the Queen tried to silence him and at length she over-reached herself. Tired of her husband, Lord Darnley, she connived at his murder, and then took the Earl of Bothwell, the man responsible for the murder, for her husband. Once more the Protestant forces took up arms, and in 1568 Mary's forces were beaten and she took flight to England, where she was eventually executed.

This event introduced another monarch who was only an infant. Mary had left behind her son of two years, James VI (and the future James I of England). Although he had been baptized according to Catholic rites, it was around James that Protestant hopes for the future now settled, and his education was in Protestant hands. In the meantime another regent, the Protestant Earl of Moray, was appointed. Yet opposition was by no means over. Large numbers still adhered to the old religion. A party for the Queen still continued to hold Edinburgh Castle — almost within gunshot of Knox's church of St Giles.

---

intermingled in the Reformation. There were motives besides the gospel for men to turn Protestant, not least the existence of wealthy church lands and their revenues that were now defenceless before the nobility. Knox understood this very well.

Moray was assassinated in 1570, and the next year things were so precarious in Edinburgh that Knox was forced to go to St Andrews with his family. In that place, we are told, 'the majority of the university had steadily set themselves against Knox and his preaching'.[30] Knox had good reason to say:

> Above all things, preserve the Kirk from the bondage of the Universities. Persuade them to rule peaceably, and order their schools in Christ; but subject never the pulpit to their judgment.[31]

In 1572, the year of his death, when he was back in Edinburgh, the majority of the nobility in the land remained against him. Old associates had deserted him, including Kirkcaldy of Grange, the man who held Edinburgh Castle for the Queen. Knox was thankful that the gospel was being preached across Scotland but he had no illusions that a nation had turned to God. In one of his last recorded prayers we hear him saying: 'Be merciful to us, and suffer not Satan utterly to prevail against thy little flock within this realm.'[32] It was one thing to see the Roman Church formally overthrown and quite another to bring such change as would

[30] Hume Brown, *Knox,* vol. 2, p. 277.
[31] Laing, *Knox,* vol. 6, p. 619.
[32] *Ibid.,* p. 569.

establish a national church that was truly evangelical and reformed.

Knox the Man

Something must be said on Knox as a person. For his appearance we have the words of a contemporary who tells us he was slightly under medium height, with black hair, broad shoulders, florid complexion and a beard 'a span and a half long'. His forehead stood out over his blue-grey eyes, with their keen gaze. In his face there was a natural dignity and majesty, and in anger there was an air of command.

In his temperament Knox was not, as someone has said, a kind of human cannonball, inflexible and insensitive. On the contrary, he could recognize situations where the exercise of moderation was a Christian duty. He did not approve, for instance, of those who advocated secession from the Church of England in the 1560s because of differences not essential to salvation. 'God forbid', he wrote to them, 'that we should damn all for false prophets and heretics that agree not with us in apparel and other opinions, who yet preach the substance of doctrine and salvation in Christ Jesus.'[33]

[33] Quoted by Peter Lorimer, *John Knox and the Church of*

William Croft Dickinson accused Knox of 'a narrow hate that diminishes the stature of the man'.[34] Certainly he was possessed of an indignation against all that dishonoured God, and while it may be questioned whether this was always rightly directed, he did not exempt himself from the same judgment. In his last publication he confessed: 'In youth, middle age, and now after many battles, I find nothing in me but vanity and corruption.'[35]

From such words it should not be deduced that Knox's prevailing spirit was one of gloom. He knew comfort and joy from the reality which Wishart expressed in the words, 'God is friendly minded towards sinners.' Thus Knox could say, 'I am assured my manifold rebellions are defaced, my grievous sins purged, and my soul made the tabernacle of thy godly majesty.' From this assurance came the tenderness with which he sought to comfort others in spiritual distress. In contrast to the representation some give of him as a man who chiefly thundered out judgments, he describes himself rather as an assistant at a banquet of blessing where the Saviour himself is the host:

England (London: King, 1875), p. 234. The 'apparel' issue concerned the disagreement over the dress of ministers.

[34] Dickinson, Knox's History, vol. 1, p. lxxiii.

[35] Laing, Knox, vol. 6, p. 483.

I was one of that number whom God appointed
to receive that bread (as it was broken by
Christ Jesus) to distribute and give the same
to such as he had called to this banquet
. . . Of this I am assured, that the benediction of Christ so multiplied the portion that I
received of his hands, that during that banquet
(this I write to the praise of his name, and to
the accusation of mine own unthankfulness)
the bread never failed when the hungry soul
craved or cried for food; and at the end of
the banquet, mine own conscience beareth
witness, that my hands gathered up the crumbs
that were left in such abundance that my
basket was full among the rest.[36]

Knox was a man of deep feeling. Listen to these
words, written to Ann Lock from St Andrews at
the end of his first year back in Scotland, December
31, 1559:

I have read the cares and temptations of
Moses, and some times I supposed myself to
be well practised in such dangerous battles.
But, alas! I now perceive that all my practice
before was but mere speculation; for one day
of troubles, since my last arrival in Scotland,
has more pierced my heart than all the tor-
ments of the galleys did the space of nineteen

[36] *Ibid.*, vol. 3, pp. 268–9.

months; for that torment, for the most part, did touch the body, but this pierces the soul and inward affections.[37]

We would know more of the personal side of Knox if his correspondence with his wife had survived. Marjory Bowes and her mother escaped from England to join Marjory's husband in Geneva during the Marian persecution. Soon after Knox returned to Scotland in 1559 she followed with their two small boys. Besides caring for the family, she acted as his secretary. In the traumatic days when she made a home in Scotland it is not surprising to read that she suffered much from sleeplessness. He wrote from St Andrews on the last day of 1559: 'The rest of my wife has been so unrestful since her arriving here, that scarcely could she tell on the morrow, what she wrote at night.'[38] Still only in her twenties, the health of Marjory Knox failed. Before the end of 1560 she was dead, and Knox had to continue alone. Hearing the news, John Calvin wrote to Knox in a letter of condolence, 'You found a wife whose like is not found everywhere.' In a letter to Christopher Goodman, the Genevan reformer also commented: 'Although

[37] *Ibid.*, vol. 6, p. 104.
[38] *Ibid.*, vol. 6, p. 104.

I am not a little grieved that our brother Knox has been deprived of the most delightful of wives, yet I rejoice that he has not been so afflicted by her death as to cease his active labours in the cause of Christ and the Church.'[39]

Three years later Knox remarried, and by his second wife, Margaret Stewart (who was seventeen, and he about forty-nine), there were three children, all girls. The youngest of the three, Elizabeth, was to marry John Welsh of Ayr, and as Thomas M'Crie says, she 'seems to have inherited no inconsiderable portion of her father's spirit'.[40]

Many false charges were made against Knox, but no one attempted to accuse him of making money from the gospel. He never owned a house, and moved frequently from one rented building to another, at times harassed by his landlord. The house on the High Street, Edinburgh, where tradition says he died, was owned by a goldsmith named James Mossman—a resolute supporter of Mary and the Catholic cause, who had taken refuge in

[39] *Ibid.*, vol. 6, pp. 124-5.
[40] Thomas M'Crie, *Life of John Knox* (Edinburgh: Blackwood, 1873), p. 294. It was M'Crie's *Life of Knox* that began the recovery of the reformer's reputation on its first publication in 1811. It remains in print today (Free Presbyterian Publications, Glasgow).

Edinburgh Castle. In Knox's last Will and Testament, while his books were valued at £130 Scots, his other household effects only amounted to £30. Hume Brown has illustrated the value of these sums by comparing them with the amount that Queen Mary once gave to her secretary, David Rizzio, namely, £200 for the repair of his chamber.[41]

What We May Learn from Knox

1. In the church situation of today there is an advantage that Knox did not have. Unlike him, we are the inheritors of traditions, and many of them good ones. In the sixteenth century the reformers had few traditions with which to work. Instead they had to break an existing mould and put another in its place. A similar task faces the church in some countries today, while in Britain we have the aid of nearly five hundred years of Protestant history. Yet while these traditions are an advantage in some respects, they can also be a danger. In an anxiety to conserve them we may lose the freedom and

[41] Hume Brown, *Knox,* vol. 2, pp. 315–6n. It is not easy to relate the sums quoted with those given by Jasper Ridley who, in the values of 1968, reckoned that Knox left assets worth about £45,000, with some £25,000 of that amount owing to him in debts. Jasper Ridley, *John Knox* (Oxford: Clarendon Press, 1968), p. 518.

flexibility to make necessary adjustments in the life of the church. We also face the danger that contemporary contempt for tradition may incline us to the opposite extreme, so that we think it needful to retain every practice that time has honoured.

Knox is not often thought of as an example of fresh and innovative thinking in the life of the church. That is certainly correct if we are thinking of the great issues of truth upon which salvation itself depends. But there are other areas where it may well be legitimate to adapt our plans and organization to the circumstances of the hour, and Knox did this at several points. In other words, he did not believe that what was later to be called the 'regulative principle of Scripture' has so determined everything in the church that we have one permanent blueprint that covers all. How often the Lord's Supper should be observed is a case in point. Scripture does not lay down precisely how often it is to be received. Once a month, the church at Geneva decided; 'four times in the year we think sufficient', said Knox and his brethren in 1560. Why the difference? The answer was one of expediency rather than of scriptural principle, 'that the superstition of the times may be avoided as far as may'.[42]

---

[42] Laing, *Knox*, vol. 2, p. 239. The General Assembly of 1562

Whether expediency was wise in this instance may well be questioned, and there are other questions on which the flexibility of the Scottish reformers is better illustrated. What part does the church member, who is not an elder or minister, play in the active life of the church? Is any part expected of him other than attending services? The 'privy kirks', through which the spiritual Reformation in Scotland came into being, certainly thought so. In the years of the hidden advance of the gospel, there were no 'church officers', only merchants, bakers, butchers, maltmen and such-like people who could speak from their hearts, exhort, and read the Scriptures to one another even though it might cost their lives. When regular churches were formed, as they were from 1559, this pattern had proved too valuable to be wholly dispensed with. Thus a group of people, whom the Book of Discipline of 1560 called 'Readers', was encouraged to continue. 'Their duty', writes David Laing, the

---

deemed that twice a year was sufficient in rural congregations. Despite protest against the infrequency of the observation of the Lord's Supper, including that of the eighteenth-century evangelical leader, John Erskine ('On frequent Communicating', *Theological Dissertations* [Edinburgh, 1806], pp. 267–339), the tradition still persists in some of the Scottish churches.

editor of Knox's writings, 'was limited to reading the Scriptures and common prayers, with liberty, when qualified, to explain the Scriptures read, and exhort the people—hence the name Exhorter.'[43]

This is not all. Once a week, the Book of Discipline laid down, there should be held in towns a meeting similar to what is described in 1 Corinthians, chapter 14, at which 'every man shall have liberty to utter and declare his mind and knowledge to the comfort and edification of the Church . . . These exercises, we say, are things most necessary to the Church of God this day in Scotland; for thereby shall the Church have judgment and knowledge of the graces, gifts, and utterances of every man within their own body.' Rules were recorded for the meeting to be edifying, there was to be 'no invective' and 'exhortations or admonitions' must be short. The principle was that Christians are to be 'willing to communicate the gifts and spiritual graces of God with their brethren . . . For no man may be permitted to live as best pleases him within the Church of God.'[44]

[43] Laing, *Knox,* vol. 6, p. 386.

[44] *Ibid.,* vol. 2, pp. 142–5. Too often a correct insistence on the office of the minister of the Word was to lead to the form of clericalism against which George Gillespie protested

The Scripture does not lay down how men are to be called into the office of Preacher. The reformers regarded the office of Readers and Exhorters, and the weekly Exercises (or Prophesyings, as they were called), as a valuable means of proving a man's gifts. The idea that a man may be trained for the ministry and licensed before there is any real proof of his gifts was unthinkable to them.

We are not only dependent on the Book of Discipline to know Knox's view on the need for meetings where all men might speak. He urges the very same thing in his 'Letter of Wholesome Counsel' sent to the brethren in Scotland in July 1556, where he says about these meetings, 'If any brother have exhortation, question, or doubt, let him not fear to speak or move the same, so that he do it with moderation, either to edify or to be edified.'[45]

Illustrations of Knox's willingness to be innovative do not stop here. He was ready to lend his authority to the work of the men called

in the 1640s: 'The name of clergy appropriate to ministers, is full of pride and vain-glory, and hath made the holy people of God to be despised.' *Assertion of the Government of the Church of Scotland*, p. 9, in *The Presbyterian's Armoury*, vol. 1, *Works of George Gillespie* (Edinburgh: Ogle, Oliver and Boyd, 1846).

[45] Laing, *Knox*, vol. 4, p. 138.

Superintendents. Was he compromising the regulative principle in so doing? No, the Superintendents were simply ministers, they held no higher office. But at a time when preaching was widely needed and able men were few, it was decided that some of the brethren should itinerate, planting new churches and helping existing ones. The innovation claimed no express Scripture warrant but was a good expedient for the situation which confronted them. In some ways the Superintendents resembled the travelling preachers who were to be so effective in Methodism two centuries later.

Knox and the Book of Discipline teach us that fresh thinking is sometimes needed for the advancement of the gospel. The contemporary church scene demands it. Not all our traditions are of the same value. In Scotland today the organized church is viewed with almost the same sort of disdain with which the Church of Rome was viewed before the Reformation. We have church buildings, but too often the people do not come in. The Scots reformers would advise us that, along with the truth of the gospel, we need more flexibility; and the aim of flexibility should be that the church as a whole becomes a missionary force.

2. If it were to be asked what is the recurring theme in Knox's words and writings the answer is perhaps a surprising one. Sometimes he could be severe, and sometimes extreme. Given the days and the harshness of the persecution he witnessed it would be understandable if these elements had preponderated in his ministry. But his keynote was of another kind altogether. From the first years that we have anything from his pen, we find him engaged in *a ministry of encouragement*. It forms the substance of his many letters to his mother-in-law. He handles the doctrines of election and justification as causes for bright joy in believers. 'Your imperfection shall have no power to damn you', he writes to Mrs Bowes, 'for Christ's perfection is reputed to be yours by faith, which you have in his blood.'[46] 'God has received already at the hands of his only Son all that is due for our sins, and so cannot his justice require or crave any more of us, other satisfaction or recompence for our sins.'[47] He writes to the believers facing suffering and possible death in the reign of Mary Tudor, likening their situation to that of the disciples in the tempest on the lake of Galilee. He says, 'Be not moved from

[46] *Ibid.*, vol. 6, p. 519.
[47] *Ibid.*, vol. 3, p. 342.

the sure foundation of your faith. For albeit Christ Jesus be absent from you (as he was from his disciples in that great storm) by his bodily presence, yet he is present by his mighty power and grace . . . and yet he is full of pity and compassion.'[48] Or again he writes:

Stand with Christ Jesus in this day of his battle, which shall be short and the victory everlasting! For the Lord himself shall come in our defence with his mighty power; He shall give us the victory when the battle is most strong; and He shall turn our tears into everlasting joy.[49]

3. One thing stands out above all else in the life of John Knox. At many different points in his life we have the comment of individuals who saw him, and the testimony most frequently repeated has to do with one point, namely, *the power of his preaching*. One of the first times we hear of Knox's ministry is in a letter of Utenhovius, writing from London to Bullinger in Zurich, on October 12, 1552. He reported how a stranger in London has suddenly caught the public attention:

[48] *Ibid.*, vol. 3, p. 287.
[49] *Ibid.*, vol. 3, p. 215.

Some disputes have arisen within these few days among the bishops, in consequence of a sermon of a pious preacher, chaplain to the duke of Northumberland, preached by him before the King and Council, in which he inveighed with great freedom against kneeling at the Lord's Supper, which is still retained here by the English. This good man, however, a Scotsman by nation, has so wrought upon the minds of many persons, that we may hope some good to the Church will at length arise from it.[50]

Another such momentous occasion came seven years later, at Stirling on Wednesday, November 8, 1559. The Protestant forces of the Lords of the Congregation had been beaten by the French outside Edinburgh and had retreated from the city by night, with insults shouted at them as they departed: 'We would never have believed', wrote Knox, 'that our natural countrymen and women could have wished our destruction so unmercifully, and have so rejoiced in our adversity.' They marched to Stirling and regathered, helpless and demoralized, except for one man. It was at this low point that Knox preached to them from Psalm 80, 'Turn us again, O God of hosts, and cause thy face

[50] Hume Brown, *Knox*, vol. 1, p. 126.

to shine; and we shall be saved.' For years to come men spoke of the effect of that one sermon. The listeners acted like men brought back from the dead. The words of the English ambassador, spoken on a later occasion, describe it perfectly: 'The voice of one man is able in one hour to put more life in us than five hundred trumpets continually blustering in our ears.'[51]

One other account of such preaching is too memorable to be omitted. As already noted, in July 1571 the Queen's party had such power in Edinburgh that Knox was forced to stay in St Andrews for thirteen months. A student there at the time was fifteen-year-old James Melville, and he would see Knox walking to church from the old priory, a staff in one hand and held under his other armpit by a friend, with furs wrapped round his neck. It was the year before his death and his strength was gone. Melville wrote in his autobiography:

> Of all the benefits I had that year [1571] was the coming of that most notable prophet and apostle of our nation, Mr John Knox, to St Andrews . . . I heard him teach there the prophecy of Daniel that summer and winter

[51] A. Taylor Innes, *John Knox* (Edinburgh: Oliphant, 1896), pp. 89–90.

following. I had my pen and my little book, and took away such things as I could comprehend. In the opening up of his text he was moderate the space of an half hour; but when he entered to application, he made me so grew [shudder] and tremble, that I could not hold a pen to write.[52]

Melville says further that Knox had to be lifted up into the pulpit

where it behoved him to lean at his first entry; but before he had done with his sermon he was so active and vigorous, that he was like to ding that pulpit in blads and fly out of it![53]

What made Knox this kind of preacher? He had natural gifts, of course, but not more than some others who never made such an impression. 'I am not a good orator in my own cause,' he once wrote to his mother-in-law.[54] When it came to preaching it was not his own cause. 'It hath pleased God of his superabundant grace to make me, most wretched of many thousands, a witness, minister and preacher.' His authority came from the conviction that preaching is God's work, the message is his

[52] *The Autobiography and Diary of Mr. James Melvill*, ed. Robert Pitcairn (Edinburgh: Wodrow Soc., 1842), p. 26.

[53] *Ibid.*, p. 33.

[54] Laing, *Knox*, vol. 3, p. 378.

word, and he was sure the Holy Spirit would honour it. This was the certainty which possessed him. I do not say there were not moments of doubt, but at the great crises the Holy Spirit so filled him that nothing could deter him, and the result was the transformations that occurred even in the most unpromising and hostile circumstances.

In the summer of 1559, when he first returned to St Andrews, warning was sent to him by the bishop that if he dared to preach the next Sunday there would be a dozen hand guns discharged in his face. His friends advised delay but he went ahead and took for his text Christ driving the buyers and sellers out of the temple. The famous painting of the scene by Sir David Wilkie captured something of that day, June 11, 1559, and the effect of it at the time can be seen in the number of priests of the Roman Church who confessed the faith.

It was due to a similar crisis that we have the only sermon Knox ever prepared for publication. The text was Isaiah 26:13–21 and the sermon was preached on August 19, 1565 in St Giles. The previous month Lord Darnley had married Queen Mary and was declared King. Darnley has been described as a man who could be either Catholic or Protestant as it suited him; sometimes he went

JOHN KNOX AND THE REFORMATION

'to mass with the Queen and sometimes attended the Reformed sermons'.[55] On this particular Sunday he sat listening on a throne in St Giles and, while he was not directly mentioned in the sermon, it so infuriated him that Knox was instantly summoned before the Privy Council and forbidden to preach while the King and Queen were in town. Part of Knox's response was to write down the sermon as fully as he could remember it. It is the only Knox sermon that has survived, and in its conclusion he has these memorable sentences:

> Let us now humble ourselves in the presence of our God, and, from the bottom of our hearts, let us desire him to assist us with the power of his Holy Spirit . . . that albeit we see his Church so diminished, that it shall appear to be brought, as it were, to utter extermination, that yet we may be assured that in our God there is power and will to increase the number of his chosen, even while they be enlarged to the uttermost coasts of the earth.

Then, at the end of the sermon Knox added this postscript which was also printed:

> Lord, into thy hands I commend my spirit; for the terrible roaring of guns, and the noise of

[55] *Ibid.*, vol. 6, p. 223.

armour, do so pierce my heart, that my soul thirsts to depart. The last of August 1565, at four at afternoon, written indigestly, but yet truly so far as memory would serve.[56]

The only true explanation of Knox's preaching is in words he applied to others of his fellow countrymen, 'God gave his Holy Spirit to simple men in great abundance.'[57] To read Knox is to be convicted of the smallness of our faith in the power of the Word of God. Unbelief has had too much influence upon us. The modern church needs to relearn the words of 2 Corinthians 4:13: 'We having the same spirit of faith, according as it is written, I believed, and therefore have I spoken; we also believe, and therefore speak.'

4. The history of the church at the time of the Reformation is a singular reminder to us of how *God is in history*. Christ is in the church and on the throne—directing and governing all persons and all events. Standing where we do in time we see Knox's faith in this fact verified, but it was another thing for him to see it in the midst of poverty, when good men were being put to death, and when he endured his twelve years of exile. Yet the truth is

---

[56] *Ibid.,* vol. 6, p. 673.
[57] *Ibid.,* vol. 1, p. 101.

that it was the storm of persecution which scattered Christians that was the very means God used to advance his purposes. If Knox had never been a refugee in England he would never have formed the friendships which became so significant in drawing the two long-hostile nations together.

When Knox came back to Scotland in 1559, with his English wife and the English tongue, the world for him was a much bigger place. And it was the exile of Knox and others in Calvin's city which gave Britain the Geneva Bible, the version that was to be the most used through much of the next hundred years. So by persecution the gospel advanced, and it was the means by which God forged an international vision and co-operation among his people. Samuel Rutherford surely stated history accurately when he wrote:

> Christ hath a great design of free grace to these lands; but his wheels must move over mountains and rocks. He never yet wooed a bride on earth, but in blood, in fire, and in the wilderness.[58]

[58] David Hay Fleming, *Critical Reviews Relating Chiefly to Scotland* (London: Hodder and Stoughton, 1912), p. 167.

In the spring of 1572, while Knox was still in St Andrews, there was a marked decline in his health, yet in August he was able to return to Edinburgh and, after thirteen months absence, preach again in the pulpit of St Giles. But the vast congregation could no longer hear his now feeble voice, and thereafter he chose the pulpit of the much smaller Tolbooth Church, where he began to preach on the crucifixion on 21 September. The English ambassador reported on 6 October, 'John Knox is now so feeble as scarce can he stand alone, or speak to be heard of any audience.' Yet he was able, on Sunday, 9 November, to preach at the installation of his successor, James Lawson. It was the last time he was to leave his home. The following Thursday he had to lay aside reading and on the Friday, confused which day it was, he declared he meant to go to church and to preach on the resurrection of Christ. A week later, with increasing difficulty in breathing, he ordered his coffin to be made and waking hours were now spent in hearing Scripture read (especially Isaiah 53, John 17, and Ephesians), saying good-bye to friends, and speaking brief words of testimony and prayer: 'Live in Christ. Live in Christ, and then flesh need not fear death—Lord, grant true pastors to thy Church, that purity of doctrine may be maintained.'

On Monday, November 24, 1572, he insisted on rising and dressing but within half an hour he had to be put back to bed. To the question of a friend, Had he any pain?, he replied: 'It is no painful pain, but such a pain as shall soon, I trust, put an end to the battle.' There was further intermittent conversation that day and a last reading of 1 Corinthians 15 at which he exclaimed, 'Is not that a comfortable chapter?' About eleven o'clock that evening, he said, 'Now it is come', and, lifting up one hand, he passed through his final conflict in peace. In the words of his secretary, Richard Bannatyne:

> In this manner departed this man of God: the light of Scotland, the comfort of the Church within the same, the mirror of godliness, and pattern and example of all true ministers.

Support the work of the Trust and keep up-to-date with all our latest publications too by subscribing to *The Banner of Truth* magazine. Available in paper and electronic formats, it is full of interesting articles, book reviews, news and comment. For details about how to receive the magazine, and for more information about all our publications, please visit our website:

www.banneroftruth.co.uk